ALASKA
BUSH COP
The Beginning

A.W. "ANDY" ANDERSON
ALASKA'S LONGEST SERVING POLICE CHIEF—RETIRED

BOOK ONE

ALASKA BUSH COP

The Begining

A.W. "Andy" Anderson
ALASKA'S LONGEST SERVING POLICE CHIEF—RETIRED

To: Mary & Lois,
I hope you enjoy the book.

Andy Anderson

PUBLICATION
CONSULTANTS
We Believe In The Power Of Authors

PO Box 221974 Anchorage, Alaska 99522-1974
books@publicationconsultants.com—www.publicationconsultants.com

ISBN Number: 978-1-59433-905-9
eBook ISBN Number: 978-1-59433-906-6

Library of Congress Number: 2019917619

Manufactured in the United States of America

DEDICATION

Alaska Bush Cop: The Beginning,
is dedicated in loving memory of
my wife Ann, and to my daughter Donica Mae,
and to my grandson, Westin Allen Johnson, the
two most important people in my life.

Acknowledgment

I publicly thank Kevin Vandegriff
for all his encouragement in the writing of this book
and for all the hours he spent in its editing. His
expertise is greatly appreciated.

OTHER BOOKS BY
A.W. "ANDY" ANDERSON

Ramblings of Alaskan Bush Poet
A Common Man's Stories Through Rhyme

Before The Badge
Growing Up In Alaska--Short Stories

TABLE OF CONTENTS

INTRODUCTION

I n writing *Alaska Bush Cop*, it is my intention to convey the activities and operations of a small one to two-man Police Department in a small Alaskan bush community. The incidents, investigations, and activities outlined in this book all took place during my nearly 32-year police career as the chief of police for the city of Seldovia, Alaska. When I was hired for the position, I had no police training or any past experience in law enforcement of any kind. To say I was underqualified at the time, to hold any position in law enforcement, let alone that of a chief of police, would be a gross understatement. I was hired to police Seldovia on a temporary basis for a six-week period, or until the city manager could find someone interested in filling the position on a permanent basis. Gary Gunkel, who had held the position for the previous five years, had quit in the spring of that year. Leonard Lusk, a local school teacher, had filled in for the summer, but returned to his duties at Susan B. English School in the fall.

Since Seldovia is a small area, and everyone is acquainted, if not related, I have decided to give most of the people mentioned in this book fictitious names, if names are required at all. I will, however, use names of close friends and those I worked with, unless they have asked me to withhold their names. The cases, the investigations, and the activities I write about, are based on factual events. I will be referencing my daily logbooks and other materials that I generated during the course of my career. In researching my daily logbooks, I discovered

I was very lax in the records keeping department for the first few years but, after going to the Alaska State Trooper Academy in Sitka Alaska, I became much more proficient in this area. For that first two to three years, I will be depending more on memory than on actual notes or reports. I have included many of the investigations and activities that I hope you will find interesting or entertaining.

It is possible that some local residents who read my description of an event will be able to identify some of the unnamed or fictionally named people due to the circumstances surrounding the specific case. This book is not intended to offend anyone, only to report the actual occurrences in the manner in which they occurred during my tenure as chief of police for the city of Seldovia, Alaska. I'm sure the reader will find the number and types of responses that actually took place in such a small community surprising. It is my hope that my descriptions of the events will be enlightening and informative, as well as entertaining.

THE CITY OF SELDOVIA

To understand my duties as a police chief, it's important you understand a little about the logistics of the place where I served. Seldovia is a small first-class Alaska City located on the Southern Kenai Peninsula, approximately 14 miles south of Homer, on the east side of Kachemak Bay. We're located approximately 160 miles, as the crow flies, south of Anchorage. Seldovia is accessible only by air or water, and no roads connect us with the Alaska road system.

In 1979, Seldovia had approximately 800 residents, and there were three bars, two liquor stores, two grocery stores, and a fish processing plant. The two stores handled food supplies as well as mercantile items. We had, and still have, one fuel company, who keeps us supplied with necessary petroleum products as well as some hardware items. Logging, commercial fishing, and the fish processing plant were the major industries in the area at the time, and Seldovia was a very active and busy community.

The 330-foot-long Alaska State Ferry, Tustumena, serves our area, bringing in passengers, vehicles, and most of our freight and building materials, and is an extension of the Alaska Road System. It has been serving our community since 1964 and still continues today, some 55 years later.

Prior to the 1964 earthquake, Seldovia had been a very busy port with four onshore canneries, and, occasionally, a floating processor or two, where king crab, salmon, and shrimp were all processed. Due to the 1964 earthquake, the landmass in and around Seldovia sunk four to six feet, depending on who you talk to. With Seldovia being a boardwalk town built on the waterfront, the larger high tides would cover the boardwalk and enter the homes and buildings located on the Main Street, flooding the entire waterfront. Due to the health hazards, which were of great concern, the boardwalk was removed, and all the canneries and structures on Main Street were torn down. Following the demolition of the waterfront properties, only one cannery rebuilt its operation. They bought and processed fish products. The loss of three of the four canneries caused the population of Seldovia to decrease considerably. Many families, who depended on fishing for a living, moved to other ports. In August of 1979, when I was sworn into office, the city was still very active and certainly in need of a police presence. It was during this time that I began my career as a police chief for the city of Seldovia.

THE MAN THEY CALLED CHIEF

I never planned a career in law enforcement and never really aspired to be a police officer. I didn't even have a high school diploma when I took the position. During my teenage years, I couldn't see the benefit of higher education, so I quit school and went to work, wanting to get into the workplace and earn some money. On more than one occasion over the years, I have felt that a high school education would certainly have made life a lot easier. After taking the chief's position, I went back to school, studied and obtained my GED.

I had also been in a farming accident when I was seven years old, which left me with sight in only one eye, a condition that would normally keep a person from even being considered in a career in law enforcement. I have also fought a weight problem most of my life, and that too is something that is not conducive to becoming a police officer. So, you ask, how did an under-educated, one-eyed, overweight 33-year-old man become a police officer and continue in that occupation for nearly thirty-two years, setting a record for the longest-serving police chief for any city in Alaska history?

I have often thought about this myself and can only say that in the seventies, the standards for the position of chief of police were not held to the same criterion and restrictions by the Alaska Police Standards Council (APSC) as was a new hire applying for a police patrolman's position. The APSC must have felt that the chief of police position was, for the most part, an administrative position which, in most departments, is true. Most chiefs of police have worked their way up through the ranks and have a good understanding of what the position requires. Most chief's positions are also administrative in nature, with very little, if any, actual hands-on police actions being taken by the chief personally. Regardless of the reasons, this one-eyed, overweight, under-educated man could legally serve as a police chief. Today, most probably, the laws and regulations have changed and have become much more restrictive, preventing someone like myself from ever being considered for such a position.

The Seldovia Police Department was a one-man police department for most of my career, and this resulted in the chief of police doing everything. The title of "Chief" was just that, a title only. When money was available in the city budget, a patrol officer, and/or some clerical help, would be hired, but when the patrol officer or the secretary decided to move on, the City Council was always hesitant to refill the position. This was a problem throughout my entire career. We would have a two-man department for a time, or clerical help for a while, then it would revert to a one-man department when the patrol officer, or the clerical help, left. Most of the patrol officers left to join a department where they would have a chance for advancement. You couldn't blame the officer for wanting to work in a department where he had a chance of working his way up the ladder. It seemed replacing an officer, or the clerical assistant, was always a budgetary concern, and it appeared to me the police department always caught the brunt of any deficit. In a one-man department, the one officer, regardless of rank, took all the calls, be it enforcing dog ordinances, working traffic control, conducting investigations, doing secretarial duties, being a counselor when called on, or for a myriad of other responsibilities that fell within the job description. Even in a two-man department, the chief of police still responded to all the calls taken on his shift, and would be on standby to assist a patrol officer on any dangerous calls that came in on the chief's off-shift. I found the chief of police position to be much more than I could have ever envisioned. I literally had no idea what I was getting myself into.

Sworn to Protect and Serve

My Police career began on August 9, 1979, when Don Caswell, city manager for the city of Seldovia, found the city without a police presence. Mr. Caswell told me he needed someone to fill the position temporarily, for a period of six weeks, or until a permanent employee could be hired for the position. I was between jobs at the time, having just finished commercial fishing for halibut from my skiff. I discussed the job offer with my wife and, not having any other employment opportunities available at the time, and not wanting to have to travel away from home again for employment, we decided I should take this temporary position.

My wife was born and raised in Seldovia, and the majority of her relatives still lived here. I had moved to Seldovia on May 1, 1964, as a teenager, and for the next fifteen years, I had worked in a number of different occupations, so we were both well known in the community.

To say I had mixed emotions, as I walked down to the city office to pick up the patrol car and be sworn in, would be a gross understatement. Upon my arrival at the city office, Mr. Caswell took me into his office, where we could talk in private. He said he wanted me to be fully aware of the position I was about to take up. He said the job consisted of my being available to respond at a moment's notice, twenty-four hours a day, seven days a week. I would be the only law enforcement officer on this side of Kachemak Bay, and I would be expected to enforce the laws and ordinances fairly and equally. He said the city office personnel would dispatch for me during working hours, but I would be responsible for taking all police-related telephone calls after hours, on weekends, and on holidays. The police phone would be installed at my residence and had to be manned anytime the city office was closed, he said. He told me what my wages would be, and I agreed to the stipulations. Mr. Caswell handed me keys to the city, a handheld VHF radio, keys to a Jeep station wagon, and a 38-caliber pistol, which he said belonged to the Seldovia police department. He also produced a small cardboard box with some paperwork in it, which I later learned was the total extent of the case files that had been generated by my predecessors.

Mr. Caswell told me that in his search for someone to temporarily fill the position, he had conducted a background check on me and had inquired about me locally. He said he had learned that I had lived in Seldovia for a number of years and was well acquainted with the local citizens and, for the most part, got along well with everyone. He shared that in his research he had found me to be honest and a hard worker, and the fact that I was six foot three inches tall, had a hefty build, and a reputation for being able to take care of myself, also weighed into his decision-making process. He said I had no criminal history he was aware of and that he'd checked me out through the Alaska State Troopers. My reputation preceded me, he said, so he based his decision primarily on my reputation and on my character. I was flattered, to say the least, but I honestly had some very real concerns about taking on a position of authority in Seldovia.

Elaine Giles, city clerk/treasurer, and a dear friend, administered the Oath of Office, and I was sworn in as the police chief for the city of Seldovia. I was given a badge, which I pinned to the left side of the leather vest I was wearing, and I was shown my office, which was located just down the hall from the city clerk/treasurer's office. Mr. Caswell congratulated me, shook my hand, and told me he looked forward to working with me. When I inquired about a jail facility, he smiled and jokingly asked, "What's that?" He said there was no jail or holding facility, and anyone I did arrest would have to be transported to the Homer Jail facility, regardless of the time, day, or night. He told me I would be dealing with the Homer Court regarding any criminal charges that might be brought. He then pointed to the Alaska State Statutes and the Municipal Code books located on a shelf in my office, and told me I needed to get acquainted with the criminal law in those books.

So, my career in law enforcement had begun, a position I would hold until June 30, 2011, just shy of thirty-two years later. As previously mentioned, I knew of no one in law enforcement locally, who I could call on for advice or assistance should the need arise, plus, there was no jail or holding facility. I had no idea how I would even handle an arrest if I had to make one, let alone how to ready a case for the courts.

I found myself the chief of police of a city in Alaska with no idea of what to do next. In all of my adult life, I had never felt so ill-prepared when taking on a new position. I had zero experience in record keeping and, at the time, I couldn't tell you the difference between a misdemeanor and a felony. I thought, "Wow, what in the world have I gotten myself into this time?" During my teenage years, and throughout my adult life, I had worked in many different occupations and for many different people, but I had always felt somewhat comfortable with the fact that I knew enough about the job I had been hired for, so that I could fulfill any and all duties it required. Not so as chief of police. The adjustment for me was a difficult one, to say the least. I had never been in a position of authority before, and I was not really sure how to exert that authority, and I had no idea of what lay ahead.

I had also never considered the fact that I would be viewed differently by many of my friends, just because I now wore a badge. I would very soon come to realize that some people, whom I had known for years, would react differently now, and some would actually avoid contact with me whenever possible. I had always been taught to respect authority, be it an elder, a teacher, a boss, a parent, a minister or a police officer. I assumed everyone felt this way, and I never considered I would be treated differently for no other reason than the position I now held. It would be an understatement to say I was naive. I would find out quickly that the job was much more than I could have ever envisioned. I found I was now also expected to have all the answers to any legal questions the public may have, due to the mere fact that I was now a sworn police officer. I found it ironic that the people who knew me best, and were well aware of my lack of police training, also expected me to have all the answers to any legal question they may come up with.

I do have to admit, I was enjoying the attention I was getting while I was adjusting to the idea of being the police chief. I was pretty pumped after putting on the badge. I was nervous, excited, and scared, all at the same time. Never had any other position I'd ever held brought to bear all these emotions. I was nervous because I didn't have a clue as to what I was supposed to do next in my new job, excited because I had always looked up to and respected those in this profession and would now be a part of it myself, and frightened because I had been given all this responsibility and feared I couldn't fulfill what was expected of me. I sincerely wanted to do the best job possible to gain the respect and trust of the people I was sworn to protect, even if it was for only six weeks. While all these emotions surged within me, I decided it was vitally important that I treat everyone equally when enforcing the rules and regulations, regardless of who I was dealing with. I decided right then that my motto would be that as long as I wore the badge, I would *"Treat a drunk like a preacher and a preacher like a drunk."*

I felt by treating everyone equally, I would quickly gain the trust and respect of the public, but over time, I discovered that gaining the public's trust and respect would be a daunting task, which would take a great deal of time, and an even greater effort on my part. I found trust and respect weren't things that came with a title, or something that was obtained because you were a resident or well known in the community. To earn the public's trust and respect, I had to work toward that goal daily. It would take a very, very long time, and then this trust and respect would only be shared by a portion of the population. Some people would never trust me, merely due to the fact I was a police officer. That was hard for me to accept, but the reality is sometimes difficult. Regardless, I had agreed to take on this job, and I planned to do it to the best of my ability. I intended to be honest and as fair as possible in the enforcement of the laws and regulations, regardless of who I might be dealing with. This, I vowed to myself, and throughout my career, although others may disagree, I feel I have honestly fulfilled this oath to myself.

Many times, it would have been much easier to have walked away when dealing with family or friends, and not taken any action at all, but I didn't feel I had that option. I felt I had to be totally neutral in my enforcement of the laws and ordinances. When you are acquainted with 99 percent of everyone you have contact with, it would be very easy to just look the other way when dealing with a friend, a relative or a close acquaintance. My job would have been a lot less stressful had I just looked the other way on many occasions, but I didn't feel I would be doing the job honestly if I had done so. I had taken an oath to enforce the law and to treat everyone equally, and I took that oath seriously, and it was vitally important to me that I also be true to myself.

As my career developed, my wife and I found our social life becoming less and less active, and the holidays, Thanksgiving and Christmas, became more and more quiet. I accepted this as part of the sacrifice I had to make due to my position of authority in such a small community. I was very concerned, however, with the fact that my wife and daughter were also caught up in the pettiness of all of this, and that made me angry at times. We felt some close friends and relatives weren't at all considerate or supportive of our position and that, at times, they felt they possibly should have gotten a pass because of our relationship. I believed if a person is a true friend, and/or a relative, they should never do anything that would put me in a position where I would have to make a decision that could negatively impact them. On most of these occasions, there was no decision to be made on my part anyway, only actions that had to be taken as was mandated by city, state or federal law. I did have a lot of discrepancies when it came to writing a citation but, in more serious cases, I was required to take whatever action the incident warranted. In most cases, the actions taken by the person committing the act mandated the response I was required to take. It boiled down to this: either I enforce the law fairly and equally, or not enforce it at all. I chose to enforce the law fairly, equally, and honestly, to the best of my ability.

Calling on Big Brother

I n contemplating my next move, I considered what I would have to do in order to successfully police the Seldovia area. My first decision was that I would have to have someone in law enforcement whom I could call on for advice. The only people I felt could assist me were the Alaska State Troopers (AST), so I called the Homer Post of the AST. The Alaska State Troopers shared the building and dispatch with the Homer Police Department (HPD), so when the dispatcher answered, I introduced myself and told him I was the new police chief of Seldovia, and that I needed to talk to a trooper. The dispatcher, Greg McCullough, who would become a very important part of my career and a close friend, connected me with Trooper Bruce Bayes, a man who would become my mentor and a very close friend, as well. Trooper Bayes guided me throughout my entire career. He was always there to advise and help me in the decision-making process. Through him, I met Troopers Dan Weatherly, John Adams, Tom Preshaw, and Mike Dowd, also great resources, who made themselves available for me to also call on for advice. As time went on, I was honored to meet many Alaska state troopers and officers, and dispatchers of HPD who, to this day, hold a very dear place in my heart. They all went out of their way to assist me and, Lord knows, I needed all the help I could get. Throughout my writings, I will be introducing you to these great people, who became an integral part of my life and made my career a reality.

When Trooper Bayes answered the phone, I introduced myself and told him I'd been sworn in as chief of police for Seldovia for a six-week period, and that I didn't have a clue as to what to do next. I told him I had no previous law enforcement training or experience, and that I needed someone I could call on for advice regarding any enforcement issues I would become involved in. I still recall the first words of advice Trooper Bayes shared with me. He said, and I quote, *"If something comes up, before you do anything at all, for God's sake give me a call."* I have little doubt this most probably was a statement he has regretted many times over the years. I took Trooper Bayes literally, and I called on him at all hours of the day and night for many years. I don't remember one occasion where he failed to respond to my requests for assistance. He would guide me through the decision-making process, or he would respond in-person to assist me in an investigation. I'm sure there were many times he cringed when he found it was Chief Anderson on the telephone.

Homer Police Department (HPD) also played a huge role in my career in that they took me under their wing, and Chief Mike Daugherty and his staff treated me as if I were one of their own. I became acquainted with the dispatchers and the police officers of HPD, and I found them to be a very important resource as well as great friends. Our relationship evolved over the years and continued to get better and better. The Homer Police Department, after a time, actually took over all the 911 calls for the Seldovia area; they dispatched me and my associates on police calls, and they treated us the same as if we were HPD Officers. They conducted all background, license, and warrant checks we requested, and our job could not have been done without their assistance. When I was responding to a call, I would make them aware of the response and my location, and they would do welfare checks if I did not contact them within a given period of time. I found having someone with their expertise in your corner was very comforting, and, even though you were often responding without backup, you were never alone. The dispatchers of HPD always had your back and would take whatever steps necessary to see to your safety and/or your welfare. This relationship continued all throughout my nearly 32-year career and, even though employees came and went in both HPD and AST, our relationship with both departments only became better and better. I found AST and HPD to be of vital importance in the policing of the Seldovia area, and my associates, the citizens of our community, and I benefited greatly from our relationship.

HITTING THE STREETS

The weather was warm on the ninth day of August in 1979 as I drove around town, trying to get used to the idea of being a police officer. The public, upon seeing me driving the police vehicle, would glance my way and then do a double take when they realized I was the person behind the wheel. Some people smiled while others stared, no one believing what they were seeing. I had always been a heavy equipment operator, a logger, a laborer, or a fisherman, and to view me in the capacity of a figure of authority was shocking for nearly everyone. I had a couple people flag me down and ask me what I was doing driving the police vehicle. When I informed them that I was the new chief of police, they said they couldn't believe it. I just didn't fit the mold, I guess.

I drove around Seldovia for a couple hours, trying to get the feel of being in my new position. I observed a couple stop sign violations, but I didn't feel I was ready to conduct a traffic stop. I didn't want to give the impression that I was going to be overly aggressive in enforcement issues. I wanted the citizens to get used to my being their chief of police and I wanted them to feel they were able to call on me for assistance.

After driving around, I went home to the mobile home we lived in on the north end of town. My wife and daughter welcomed me home, jokingly calling me "Chief." They too had to get used to the idea that I now held a position of authority in Seldovia. I was concerned as to how the students at my daughter Donica's school would treat her now, since her dad was the local chief. I decided to just wait and see how she handled any peer pressure due to my new position. I told my wife and daughter about the police telephone that would be installed in our home, and that it would have to be monitored anytime the city hall was closed. Donica wasn't at all excited about this, knowing she would be staying home sometimes when her mother was away from home, visiting or at some function. She was ten years old at the time and would have to accept some responsibility due to her father's employment status. I told my girls that all three of us would be impacted by my job, and we would just have to get used to the idea. We didn't have an option as long as I was chief of police.

It would be a few days before the police telephone would be installed in our residence, and until then I would be relying on any police related calls to be dispatched through City Hall.

MY FIRST INVESTIGATION

M id-morning of August 10, 1979, I received my first police related call from Elaine Giles, telling me a local fisherman wished to meet with me, and she asked if I could drop by at his residence. I told her I'd be at his residence within ten minutes.

I reached the fisherman's residence and found him waiting outside to talk to me. He reported that someone had stolen ten of his shrimp pots, which he had stored on cannery property. I asked if he'd talked to the superintendent at the cannery, and he said he had not. I told him I'd check into the matter. The pots had been stored for a couple years, he said, but upon checking yesterday, he'd found them missing.

I left the man's residence and drove to the cannery. I went into the office and told the secretary I'd like to see the superintendent. I was invited into his office, and he asked what he could do for me. I told him I'd been hired as the new chief of police, and I related the complainant's report. The superintendent told me the pots had been sold to another fisherman because they had been stored for so long that the cannery personnel thought they were abandoned. I asked how many pots had been sold, and he said there were ten pots that had been stored for over four years, and prior to selling them, they had attempted to locate the owner. He said there were no markings on the gear to indicate who owned them, and after they couldn't locate the owner, they felt it was okay to sell them. I told the superintendent that I would have the complainant drop by and see him, and they could work it out. He assured me they would make it right with the fisherman.

I drove back to the complainant's residence and told him what I'd found out. He was upset, but said he'd get in touch with the cannery. I told him the cannery superintendent had told me that the pots had been stored for over four years instead of two. I suggested he should take this fact into consideration when meeting with the cannery personnel. He thanked me, and I left feeling good, having solved my first case. I thought to myself that the job would be great if everything turned out like this case did. (Case Closed by Investigation)

CRIMINAL MISCHIEF

After leaving the fisherman's residence, I was patrolling around town when Elaine Giles again called me on the radio and told me a man living in a trailer above Wheeler's Store wanted to see me regarding some damage done to his trailer. I told Ms. Giles I would respond, and I drove to the location, arriving at approximately 1250 hours. The cannery foreman came out of the trailer when he saw me drive up. He told me he'd been sleeping, and he'd heard banging on the side of the mobile home; when he looked out the window, he saw two male teenagers walking down the hill. He did not recognize either one of them, he said, but they stopped at the bottom of the hill and were talking to a girl who was riding a horse. The complainant then showed me two broken louver type window panes on the entry door that he said the two teenagers had broken. He thought they were probably trying to break into the trailer, thinking everyone who lived there was at work. He thought something must have scared them away. He assured me that he didn't know them, and he hadn't seen the teenagers around town before.

After leaving his residence, I went to the home where the only horse in town was kept and I inquired as to who was riding the horse that morning. The daughter living there told me she was riding the horse and wondered what she had done wrong. I assured her that she had done nothing wrong, but might have witnessed something I needed to know. I asked her who the two teenagers were, who she'd stopped and talked with when she was riding her horse in the area at the bottom of Church Hill, beside the old theater building. She gave me the two boys' names; I was acquainted with both of them. She told me they were in town from one of the villages. I thanked her and left her residence.

I drove around town searching for the two and stopped to talk to the harbor master to see if they had left town in a skiff. He said their skiff was still moored in the transient area in the harbor. I continued my search for the two teenagers. When I was passing the Seldovia Lodge, I observed the two boys walking out of the building. I stopped them and asked what they were doing at the trailer on Church Hill that morning. At first, they denied any knowledge of the event, but after telling them I had a positive identification on them, they said they had just walked by the mobile home. I told them I knew they had broken two small window panes in the door of the mobile home, and asked if they were attempting to break into the trailer. They finally admitted to throwing a rock and breaking the window panes, but said they were not trying to break in. They said they were just goofing around. I told both the boys to get in the car, and I transported them to the police department.

It was my second day of being chief of police, and I really didn't know how to handle the case, so I called trooper Bayes and told him what I had going. He said I should write each teenager a citation for "Criminal Mischief 4th Degree," and that I should call the Homer Court for a court date and time for their arraignment. The two boys were both over eighteen years of age, so I didn't have to notify their parents, he said. I thanked the trooper and terminated the phone call. I called the Homer Court and told them who I was, and that I had to write two citations for "Criminal Mischief" for two teens over eighteen, and that I needed a date and time for their arraignments. After being given the date and time, I wrote the two young men's citations. This was the first time I'd written citations, and I was very thankful that the forms outlined the information that was needed.

After finishing the citations, I had both teenagers sign them. I got them to promise to appear in Homer Court on the date and time of their arraignment. After they both signed their citations, I gave them their two copies. I told both the boys that the next time something like this happened, I would be arresting them and transporting them to Homer Jail. Both assured me nothing like this would happen again; they said they were headed back to their village shortly. I released them, and they left the police department. (Case Closed by Arrest)

GETTING THE FEEL OF THINGS

Wow, two cases and both had been solved in just a matter of hours. I was really feeling good about the job I'd taken on but knew the two cases I'd solved didn't really amount to much. I knew I should "take um where I could get um," because this couldn't last, but so far, so good.

I was getting the feel of being a police officer and, so far, I was enjoying the job. To be truthful with you, most police work is pretty mundane. A dog call, a loud music complaint, a curfew violation or some petty theft occurring from time to time. I do not mean to trivialize these cases, but they are not something the reader wants to read about. Having said that, I will not be dwelling on the less exciting calls.

I found it all interesting when I first started but, over time, I did find some of the calls to be somewhat annoying. The late-night calls about a dog barking and how someone can't sleep, or a noise complaint next door and the complainant wants it quieted down. This is all part of police work and, in its own way, it is just as important as the more urgent calls. If the officer doesn't respond to the dog call or the noise complaint, it could very easily become something much more serious. The person calling wants something done to correct the problem or they wouldn't have called in the first place, and if the police don't take care of the problem, the complainant might, in his own way, deal with it. The complainant has no authority so when he/she contacts the person creating the problem, it can be taken totally different than if an officer responds. So, it has always been my feeling that, regardless of the time of day or night, and regardless of the type of complaint, all calls would be handled and done so in a professional manner. Throughout my career, I have mandated that all my patrol officers respond to a call regardless of their personal feelings. I always felt we were there to serve the public and to keep them safe even when we felt the call wasn't all that important, in our opinion.

On August 13, 1979, the telephone company contacted me and asked if this was a good time to install the police telephone in my home. I told the technician I would meet him at my residence. He installed two police phones in my residence, one beside my bed in my bedroom, the other in the living room. He left, and I told my wife that she and my daughter Donica had just become dispatchers for the Seldovia Police Department. Ann chuckled, but Donica didn't seem to be too enthused by the idea. I instructed them not to answer the phone during city business hours, unless the city failed to pick up.

What is ironic about this is that, as of April 15, 2019, my daughter celebrated her fifteenth year anniversary with the Tulalip Police Department in Washington State. She started as a dispatcher, later became dispatch supervisor, and is now responsible for all evidence gathered by the thirty-four sworn officers of the department. She still covers for dispatchers who, for various reasons, can't work their shift. She's very content in her job and loves what she does. Who would have ever guessed?

The next two to three weeks consisted of just patrolling and working traffic. I stopped people for speed, stop signs, and some licensing problems but didn't write any citations. I gave verbal warnings and made those I contacted aware that the next time it would result in a citation. I still felt I had to work into the position of police chief slowly, and not come on too strong.

DEATH INVESTIGATION

On October 7, 1979, at approximately 0910 hours, I was called to a residence to investigate an unattended death. The lady who had passed away had suffered for years with a serious kidney ailment. She had been undergoing dialysis a number of times during the week and was pretty much bedridden. I responded to the residence and found her daughter and my good friend, Gerry Willard, to be present. The daughter had found her mother and had called Mr. Willard who, in turn, had called me. Mr. Willard had been assisting the lady with her dialysis during the many weeks she had been undergoing the treatment.

Having never investigated a death before, I called the office of the Alaska State Troopers for assistance. Trooper Daniel Weatherly was available and he explained to me what was needed before I called the medical examiner (ME) to obtain a permit to move the remains. He said the ME would most probably ask me a number of questions, but I should have the full name, date of birth, a Social Security Number, and an Operator License Number of the deceased prior to calling. He said I would need the time of death, as close as we could come. I thanked Trooper Weatherly and I then started putting all the information together before calling the ME. Upon calling the ME, along with the questions trooper Weatherly told me would be asked, I was asked about any signs of foul play or any signs of forced entry or anything that indicated a struggle. After answering all his questions, the ME gave me permission to move the remains from the home. He asked which funeral home the family would be using and he further said he would be ordering an autopsy. After giving the ME all the information he required, he terminated the phone call, and we readied the body for transport. Arrangements were made with Cook Inlet Aviation to fly the remains to Homer, where the South Peninsula Memorial Chapel would have a transport vehicle waiting to move the remains to Soldotna, where the mortuary is located. They would be in touch with the ME reference the autopsy.

After loading the deceased on the aircraft at the Seldovia Airport, I returned to my office. I had now investigated my first death and was somewhat saddened by the experience. In the future, I knew I would be called on to investigate many more deaths. I was hoping I could do a good job, knowing many of the future victims would most probably be people with whom I was well acquainted. I had known this lady but not well. I wondered about the future investigations, given the emotions I experienced with this call. (Case Closed by Investigation)

BURGLARY OF THE SELDOVIA HOSPITAL

At approximately 1020 hours on November 30, 1979, I received a call from Dr. Larry Reynolds, reporting a burglary at the hospital, which had occurred sometime during the previous night. He reported that the entry door had been forced and a hasp and lock were pried off the medicine cabinet where all the drugs were stored. The doctor said his preliminary finding was that Codeine tablets, Valium tablets, injectable Valium, and syringes had been taken. I advised him not to touch anything when determining what was missing, so no evidence would be compromised.

I responded to the hospital and took photographs of the entry door that was forced and of the hasp and medicine cabinet, which showed tool marks made by the forced entry.

A list of missing items was given to me and the list included the following:

- 1 box syringes – 19 cc with 20-gauge needles
- 30 mg. Codeine pills (white in color) – Approximate 500 tablets
- 10 mg. Valium pills (blue in color) – Approximately 750 tablets
- 100 mg. injectable Valium – 2 vials – 50 mg. each.

After I surveyed the crime scene, I taped off the area where additional evidence could possibly be obtained and then I went to the Police Department. I was not schooled in the collection of evidence thus far in my career and I felt very inadequate investigating a crime scene, so I called the Alaska State Troopers for assistance. Trooper Bayes again came on the phone and told me he wouldn't be free for a few days, but could come over on December 4[h]. He told me to preserve the scene and not let anyone touch anything in the vicinity of the drug cabinet. He told me to take good pictures of any tool marks on the door which was forced and any other marks on objects that were forcibly opened. I assured the trooper we had taken good photographs and that the doctor and his wife had been told not to utilize the drug cabinet until everything was dusted for fingerprints.

On 12 February 1979, at approximately 1910 hours, I received a call from the Knight Sports Bar requesting I come down and talk with the manager. Upon arrival, the manager produced a paper with instructions on how to inject liquid Valium. The instructions were always placed inside the packaging of all liquid Valium boxes when they were packaged so, without a doubt, the directions had come from one of the two vials of liquid Valium that had been taken in the hospital burglary. The manager said a patron found the instructions in the men's bathroom. I thanked the manager and took the instructions as evidence.

Within the next two days, I was approached by three separate people, on separate occasions, telling me about an individual who was acting strangely, which was reportedly very different from what he usually was like. The man had also told two of the witnesses that he had some pills if they were interested. All three witnesses named the same person, and I talked to each of them at different times and with no one else present.

Trooper Bayes called me and told me he could not make it over to fingerprint the medicine cabinet at the hospital due to some other things that had come up, but he was sending a fingerprint kit over on the airlines, and I could attempt to collect prints. He gave me some pointers about lifting fingerprints and told me to see if I could give it a try. He apologized for not being able to come to assist me. I told him I would attempt to lift some prints but I didn't hold out much hope that I'd come up with anything that would be good for evidence.

I picked up the fingerprint kit from the airlines and responded to the hospital and attempted to find prints on and around the drug cabinet. I lifted a few prints but they didn't appear to me to be anything I could use in the investigation.

On December 7, at approximately 1020 hours, I received an anonymous call from a man, telling me about a young man who was flying out of Seldovia later in the morning; he said the young man was on his way to the States. The caller said the man was in possession of pills from the hospital burglary. He described the person in question but said he did not know his name. The caller was adamant about remaining anonymous but said he was sure the young man was in possession of some of the drugs taken in the hospital burglary. After we ended the conversation, I called the airlines the young man was reported to be traveling on, and I was given the names of people flying out of Seldovia with them. There was only one young man who fit the description, and I was personally acquainted with him. I was told by the airline's dispatcher that the young man was scheduled on the 1245 airplane.

At 1230 hours, I responded to the airport and contacted the young man who the caller had described. I told him I was conducting an investigation into the hospital burglary and I had information he was in possession of some pills that had been taken during that burglary. He denied having any pills but said he did have some marijuana and that he would give that to me. I told him I wanted to search his luggage to make sure he didn't have any pills; he was reluctant to let me search his bags. I told him he was a suspect in the burglary and, if I had to, I'd hold him as a suspect, and he wouldn't be able to continue his trip to Oregon. He finally admitted he did have some pills and he opened his luggage in my presence and extracted the marijuana, eleven Valium tablets, and one Codeine tablet. I ask him if he had committed the burglary, and he said he had nothing to do with it, but he did give me the name of the man who had sold him the Valium and the Codeine. The name matched the report I'd received from the three witnesses who had reported a man acting strangely. After taking possession of the drugs, I told the subject he could continue on his trip but, knowing he was on probation, I told him I'd be in touch with his probation officer in this regard, and he'd probably be reaching out to him in Oregon. He boarded the airplane and then left Seldovia.

I drove back to the police department and called Trooper Bayes again and told him what had developed in the case. He told me I had enough probable cause to arrest the suspect on burglary charges. He told me to bring him in and read him his Miranda warning. I was to then lay out for him what I had and then inform him that he was going down for the burglary at the hospital. I told the trooper I'd be in touch with him after I contacted the suspect to let him know how it went.

I left the police department and searched for my suspect and located him at the Seldovia Lodge. I asked him to come outside where I could talk to him, and he walked out of the lodge with me. When we got to the patrol vehicle, I told him he was under arrest for the burglary at the hospital. He denied any involvement, but I placed him in handcuffs and told him we'd discuss it at the police department. I transported him to the PD, and when we were inside the office, I took the handcuffs off. I had him take a seat and I read him his Miranda warning. He said he understood his rights and he agreed to talk with me. He denied any involvement in the burglary for a time but, after hearing the evidence I had obtained, he finally admitted to burglarizing the hospital, but he said he wasn't alone. He named another local man who he said also took part. They had shared the drugs, he said. He further told me that the drugs were now all gone. I had him tell me what all they had taken, and he named the injectable Valium, the Valium tablets, the syringes, and the Codeine pills. When asked if that was all, he said that was all he could remember. When asked what time the burglary took place, he said around 0200 hours. He told me he was intoxicated when he burglarized the hospital, and when I asked him if his partner was also intoxicated, he said he thought so but wasn't really sure.

I called the Homer Court and told them I needed an arraignment date and time for felony burglary. They gave me the date and time, and I filled out a "Promise to Appear Form" and had the suspect sign it. Because I didn't have a jail facility, I could not hold him and I would have to transport him to Homer Jail if I wanted to keep him in custody. He was a local fisherman, and I didn't think he would try to flee and, if he did, there would be an arrest warrant ordered. I explained all of this to him, and he said he understood and that he wasn't going anywhere. After he signed the form, I released him on his promise to appear for arraignment in Homer Court.

After the suspect left, I responded to the residence of the man he had named as a co-defendant. Upon contact, I told the man he was under arrest for the burglary at the hospital. He too adamantly denied any involvement as I placed him in handcuffs and transported him to the police department. Upon reaching the PD, I took the handcuffs off and told him to have a seat. I then read him his Miranda rights warning, and he also agreed to talk to me. He said he didn't know where I'd gotten my information but he had nothing to do with the burglary. He said he'd heard about it but wasn't involved. I told him his partner had given him up and had told me everything. I told him it would go a lot easier for him if he just manned up and admitted to his involvement. After a time, he did finally admit to his part in the burglary but said it was all his partner's idea. After getting a confession, I filled out a "Promise to Appear Form" and had him sign it. He was told not to leave the area, and he asked me where he could go. He was a local and wasn't going anywhere, he said. I delivered him back to his residence and told him to make sure he didn't miss his court date. He assured me he would be there.

With the assistance of the Alaska State Troopers, I was able to put the case together in written form for the district attorney. A Grand Jury was held, and I was called to testify for the first time in my career. A true bill was delivered on both the defendants, charging each of them with "Burglary Not in a Dwelling," a Class B felony.

Both suspects wound up pleading "No Contest" and were found guilty by the court. The first suspect I'd arrested had a criminal record and was sentenced to five years in jail with five years suspended. He was ordered to pay $226.29 in restitution to the hospital. He was also ordered not to consume alcohol or drugs and was further ordered to go into the Akela House for in-house alcohol/drug treatment. He was placed on probation for five years.

The second suspect was sentenced to five years in jail with five years suspended. He was further ordered to abstain from consuming alcohol, marijuana or any other drugs. He was ordered to complete eighty hours of community work service each year for the next three years and he was placed on probation for three years.

I felt pretty good about being able to solve the burglary at the hospital and sending a message to others that this kind of activity would not be tolerated in Seldovia. I hoped some would-be burglars would learn through this investigation.

But for the assistance of Trooper Bayes of AST, this case could have gone unsolved. (Case Closed by Arrest!)

BURGLARY OF THE CITY OFFICE AND STANDARD OIL

O n the morning of December 4, 1979, I received a call from the city that someone had broken into the City office during the night, and there were checks and papers thrown all over the floor. The intruders had also broken into the file safe where the city kept the money. By the city's figures, they were missing $1185 and the file cabinet, with the locked drawer, was damaged beyond repair. I responded to the city office and took pictures of the mess; I also attempted to pull some fingerprints from the file cabinet. I developed numerous fingerprints but I had no way of telling if they had any evidentiary value. So many people had been in an out of the file cabinet, it would be hard to determine the burglars from the employees. I would have to take comparison prints from everyone who had been into the files before sending the prints I developed to the AST lab. Others who had worked at the city, and then left for other employment opportunities, would also have their fingerprints on the cabinet. Hopefully, I could send my evidence to the AST lab with a suspects' list, and they could find one that matched. It was the proverbial pin in a haystack scenario. Fortunately, even though I shared an office in the same building, nothing in the police department area had been gone through. I never quite understood that.

I set up a schedule to roll fingerprints of the office personnel, and I collected some of the checks and papers that were strewn around the room in the hope that the burglar(s) were not wearing gloves at the time of their entry. I was also able to retrieve some fingerprints off the entry door to the office but, again, I had no way of knowing if the prints were evidentiary in value or not. After collecting the evidence, I went to my office.

I soon received a call from the Standard Oil Company, reporting they had been burglarized sometime during the night, as well. The owner's wife said the intruders had made entry through the back door and had then broken open the door leading into the business area from the warehouse. I told the lady I would be right over, but not to touch anything if they could avoid it.

I responded to the Standard Oil office and found both the owners present. It was evident that a lot of damage had occurred to the entry door and to the safe in the office area. The burglar(s) were not able to force the safe but they did get over $100 with $60 being in $1 bills, from the cash they kept in the desk drawer. The owners said an undetermined amount of coins was also missing, which they also kept in the desk.

As I did in the city office, I took fingerprints off the safe, the entry door, and the desk where the $100 and coins had been stored. The owners said the safe had the bulk of the money in it, and the burglar(s) could not break it open, so that cash was still intact. After the evidence was gathered, I scheduled a time for the Standard Oil employees to come to the police department where they too could be fingerprinted for comparison purposes. I then left the Standard Oil plant and returned to the Seldovia Police Department, where I started filling out the necessary paperwork that would accompany all the evidence, I would be sending to the AST lab. I would also be packaging the evidence and readying it for the mail.

Within the next couple days, all the personnel of both the city office and Standard Oil had their fingerprints rolled.

Because both the city office and Standard Oil had been burglarized on the same night, and because they were in close proximity to one another on Dock Street, it was my opinion that the same person, or persons had burglarized both businesses. I packaged up all the evidence and sent it to the AST lab, but nothing had any evidentiary value, and the two burglaries were never solved. I put out the word on the street regarding the fact that there were a number of coins that had been taken as well as the numerous $1 bills that someone would be spending. With all the work that went into the investigation and with all the evidence that was sent in for evaluation, nothing turned up. I would have loved to have solved these two crimes. (Both Cases Closed Pending Additional Leads)

BURGLARY OF THE HARBORMASTER'S OFFICE

On December 19, 1979, the harbormaster reported a burglary and theft from the harbormaster's office building, which had occurred sometime during the night of December 18. The small window on the southwest side of the building had been forced, and the metal cash box, containing $16.78, was forced open, and the money was taken. A check written to the City had been left in the cash box, but the money was gone.

It had snowed lightly during the night, and tracks were visible, which led away from the harbormaster's office in a northerly direction. The tread of the shoe resembled a waffle stomper type tread. I followed the tracks directly to a home where a local teenager lived. I knocked on the door, and the teenager opened the door, asking what I needed. I told him there had been a burglary at the harbormaster's office and I had followed tracks leading from the office straight to his front door. The young man told me he hadn't been out of the house at all during the night and it couldn't be his tracks. I ask him what kind of shoes he wore, and he showed me a pair of boots with a waffle stomper type tread. He was adamant about not leaving his residence during the night, so I told him I could prove he was innocent if he would let me fingerprint him and give me his boots for comparison with the tracks I had followed. I told him that whoever took the money from the cash box had, no doubt, picked up the check, and their fingerprints would be on it. I told him I would send the prints and shoes to the Alaska State Trooper's laboratory for comparison, and that would clear him if he was telling me the truth. He agreed to give me the boots and the fingerprints, and we responded to the police department with the boots with the waffle stomper tread.

As I took his fingerprints, I continued to try and persuade him to admit to the burglary, but he stood by his statement and repeated that he had not left his residence. I was convinced that I had my man and it was only a matter of time until the laboratory gave me the proof I needed.

After rolling his prints, I transported the teenager back to his residence and asked him one more time if he was involved in the burglary. I told him if he confessed now it would go a lot easier on him than it would if we went through the AST lab to prove his guilt. He seemed irritated and told me he had not left his residence and he wasn't going to admit to a crime he hadn't committed.

After dropping him off, I returned to the police department and started packaging the evidence for shipment to the AST lab. I thought to myself that this case had come to a conclusion rather quickly, and I felt pretty good about being able to solve it so soon.

While I was packing up the evidence, the telephone rang. It was the harbormaster, asking if I'd found the burglar yet. I told him I thought I had but would have to wait until information came back from the AST lab. He told me he had heard about a teenager that had been seen in the vicinity of his office between 0100 hours and 0130 hours last night. The teenager he mentioned was not the person I suspected of committing the crime. I thanked the harbormaster and told him I'd look into it.

Even though I felt confident I had my burglar, I felt I had to follow up every lead. I left the police department and went to my new suspect's home and asked if he'd come down to the police department. I told him I had some questions I wanted to ask him. He agreed to come down, and I then ask what kind of boots he wore. He picked up a pair of lace-up boots that had a waffle stomper tread. I asked him to bring the boots with him.

After we arrived at the police department, I read him his rights. I told him I'd be asking questions about a burglary that had occurred the previous night at the harbormaster's office. He agreed to talk to me, and I asked him if he'd been around the harbor office between 0100 hours and 0130 hours that morning. He said he'd walked by the harbor office pretty late but he was on his way home and didn't go near the building. I told him I thought he had burglarized the harbormaster's office and that I had boot impressions that were of a boot with a waffle stomper type tread. He adamantly denied any involvement. I told him I could prove his innocence if he would give me his boots and his fingerprints. I mentioned the check that had been left in the cash box when the money was taken. I explained to him that whoever took the money had certainly handled the check, so I could take his fingerprints and his boots and prove he wasn't there just by sending them to the AST lab for comparison. He fidgeted around a little and then asked me if I really thought they would get prints off the check. I told him I was 99 percent sure of it. The teenager's next words nearly knocked me off my feet. He said, "Well, I'd like to confess then. I broke in and took the money." I was not expecting a confession, and it took me totally off guard. I had already made up my mind that the first suspect I'd questioned was the guilty party.

Upon his confessing to burglarizing the harbormaster's office, I asked him if he had also broken into the City office and the Standard Oil plant. He said he had heard about the burglaries but he had nothing to do with them. I told him I was waiting for the results of the fingerprints I had sent to the AST lab to come back, and if his prints were identified, he would be in really big trouble. I told him now would be the time to man up so the district attorney could group all three burglaries together, and he would only get one sentence. I further told him that if he denied involvement in the other two burglaries, and I did get evidence indicating it was him, he would go down hard for all three burglaries. He was still adamant that he hadn't had anything to do with the other two burglaries, so I told him I'd done all I could do in giving him a chance to man up but now he was on his own.

He still denied any involvement in the other two crimes, so I had an inclination to believe him.

I arrested the eighteen-year-old for burglary and theft and, after calling the court for a date and time of his arraignment, and upon his signing a "Promise to Appear Form," I took the young man home and released him on his own recognizance, telling him not to miss his arraignment date. Following my dropping him off, I went to my first suspect's residence and returned his boots and apologized to him for suspecting him in the burglary. He said he understood and that I was just doing my job.

At the arraignment, the suspect pled guilty to a lesser charge of "Unauthorized Entry" and "Theft in the 4th degree." He was ordered to pay $50 for the damage to the window and to pay back the $16.78 that was taken from the cash box. He was then placed on probation for one year. I would find in the years ahead that the district attorney most often would reduce a felony to a misdemeanor if the suspect didn't have a criminal past.

I learned a huge lesson in this case, and it helped me considerably throughout my career. I learned to never take things for granted and that things are not always as they seem. Many times, there is considerably more to a case than meets the eye. I learned to be thorough in my investigations and not to leave a stone unturned. In a lot of cases, nothing is what it seems to be. If I had not followed up on the harbormaster's statement regarding the second suspect, when I was thinking I already had a suspect, I may never have solved this burglary/theft. (Case Closed by Arrest)

VIOLATIONS AND PETTY CRIMES

Throughout my first year of service, I investigated a number of reports of different petty crimes and violations. I called on the Alaska State Troopers many times, and they assisted me in the decision-making process and gave me pointers on how to handle certain calls and investigations. In my first few months of service, I was shocked at the number of calls and what all was included in police work.

Many of the calls consisted of alcohol-related crimes including furnishing liquor to minors, minors consuming alcohol, and alcohol-related family disputes. A report of the theft of a motor vehicle was taken as was the theft of a gill net. Two tires were reportedly slashed on a vehicle, and damage to city property was investigated. Reports of cocaine and marijuana being distributed were also taken, but the allegations could not be proven. Three reports of criminal mischief were taken with some private property being damaged. With the patrolling, the noise-related complaints regarding dogs barking, the repeated bar checks and working traffic, I was kept quite busy in my new found profession. Every day, I learned something new, and this kept the job exciting as well as interesting.

I continued to be respectful with whomever I dealt with and I was honest in my dealings. I was determined to keep with my original plan of treating everyone equally, honestly, and with respect. I found it hard at times, when I didn't necessarily respect the person I was dealing with, but I felt it was important I didn't disrespect them either.

Christmas and New Year came and went without too many issues, and I felt I had been accepted by most of the local population.

Right after the first day of the year, the city manager called me into his office and asked me how the job was going and how I was liking the work. I shared with him that I was really enjoying all the different aspects of the job and I asked him if he had a problem with what I was doing. He assured me he was happy with my work but he said he wanted me to know that he would be leaving his position as city manager in a few weeks. He said he was putting something together in Anchorage and, as soon as it came through, he'd be leaving Seldovia. I told him I was certainly disappointed to hear this, but I understood the politics of the position were fierce. He agreed, and said most city managers don't stay long in small communities because of political pressures. He then told me he wanted this kept between the two of us in that I was the only one that knew, other than his wife. I promised him I would keep it confidential, but I was still saddened by the news. At the same time, I was flattered by the fact that he had confided in me before telling anyone else. Mr. Caswell and I had a great working relationship, and I respected and admired the man that he was. I guess he felt the same about me, given the fact that he confided in me. It wasn't too many weeks later that Mr. Caswell gave the City Council his letter of resignation with a three-week notice period. I was sorry to see Don Caswell's departure and I hoped the next city manager and I would have a good working relationship, as well.

A 4-5-6 Dice Game and a Lawsuit

On January 20, 1980, I received a call from the bartender at the Seldovia Lodge reporting that a bar fight had broken out over a 4-5-6 dice gambling game, and that I needed to get there right away. The dice game is illegal and usually results in problems. In a 4-5-6 game, a person can win a lot of money very quickly but he can also lose a lot of money in a short time. The loser usually has bet a large sum of money and is always upset over his losses. Of course, this leads to other problems. Alcohol is always involved, and tempers flare.

I geared up and responded to the Lodge. When I arrived, it was pandemonium there, and everyone was yelling. A couple guys were wrestling around on the floor in the bar area, and two guys were duking it out in the dining area. I broke up the wrestling match, telling them to stop or be arrested. They stopped wrestling and both got up, trying to blame the other for the problem. I then went into the dining area and got between those two and made them stop swinging at each other. Again, I was told by each of them that the other guy was to blame for the fight. I told them I didn't care who started it but if they continued fighting, both would go to jail.

I talked to the bartender, trying to get a feel for what was really going on. I was told a 4-5-6 game was underway when a $100 check had come up missing, and someone blamed a boat crew, which was from out of town, for taking it. That was enough, combined with the alcohol, to start the fight. I got the visiting boat crew, four men, together in the dining area and was talking to them, when a local man came in and attempted to keep the fight going. I literally threw him back into the bar area and told his buddies to keep him in there. I warned him that if he came into the dining area again and started problems, he would go to jail. They must have restrained the man because I had no more problems with him.

After it quieted down somewhat, I talked with the boat owner. He told me that due to bad weather, he and his crew had stopped in Seldovia. He said they had been in town for two and a half days. I asked him if I could transport him and his crew back down to the harbor, where they could go aboard the boat and, by doing so, avoid any further problems. The man agreed and he, and three of his crew members accompanied me out of the bar. Before I left, I told the bartender to have the owner get in touch with me the next day and that it'd be better if he got in touch with me than me having to hunt him up. I wanted to confront him on allowing illegal gambling to take place on his licensed premises.

I delivered the man and his crew to the boat harbor, and he thanked me, telling me it was a good thing I had showed up when I did. He said it could have really gotten out of hand without a police presence. I told him if he needed me to call and also that it'd probably be best if he and his crew stayed aboard the boat for the night to let this all settle down.

A lot of boats seek refuge in the Seldovia Harbor when a storm is blowing in Kachemak Bay, and this storm had been going on for a few days now. There had been near gale force winds the previous day and, due to the strong gusts, we were also without telephones in town. Our telephone system works off a reflector. The telephone reflector, which is located on top of the mountain across Seldovia Bay, was moved a little by the strong gusts of wind, preventing any signals to be reflected off it. So, there was not a telephone in town that was working, and we would have to wait until the storm passed before the telephone company could repair the reflector.

Because the patrons at the Seldovia Lodge were so hyped up, I felt I should stay in the area to prevent any further problems. I cruised around and frequently drove by the Seldovia Lodge and the harbor. On one of my passes by the harbor, I observed one of our local fishermen pulling into the harbor parking lot. When he exited his vehicle, I ask where he was going. He had been at the Lodge when the problems had occurred, but I didn't know if he had been involved in the scuffle or not, nevertheless I did feel it warranted my inquiry. He told me he had to go down and check his boat, which I felt was legitimate, knowing he had a boat moored there. I decided I would wait in the harbor parking lot until he came back from checking his vessel. No more than a few minutes had passed when I heard a shot, which came from the direction of where the visiting boat was tied up. The local fisherman was coming up the boat ramp at the time and he yelled out that he was hit in the leg. I was visiting with an EMT, who was also the fire chief, Dean Ihrie, in the parking lot at the time, and he also heard the shot and heard the fisherman yell out. I told the fisherman to let Mr. Ihrie check him but he refused, stating he was fine. I assumed at that point that he had not been hit and I asked what had happened. He said he'd gone down to talk to the crew on the boat, and they had gotten into a fight, and he'd hit the owner up alongside the head.

At this point, had I been schooled in law enforcement and not just policing through common sense, I would have detained the fisherman for assaulting the visiting boat owner. I was, however, more in the frame of mind that I had to keep both the local citizens and the visiting crew safe, and it was evident to me that the only way to accomplish this goal was to separate the two entities. To ensure everyone stayed safe, there could be no contact from either source.

The shot sounded like it had come from a shotgun, not a rifle, and a shotgun pellet could not have reached the harbor ramp from where the visiting boat was moored, so I strongly believed the local fisherman was lying about being hit in the leg. The local man left, and I called on three people to come to the harbor to assist me. We were using CB radios at the time, and I called two men and asked them to bring shotguns. I asked the third man to bring a rifle. I told them to meet me at the Seldovia Harbor. I had no idea what we would be walking into after having heard a shot come from what I believed to be the visiting vessel. I was not going to take any chances. I felt a show of force would likely keep anything more from happening.

All three men showed up within half an hour of my calling. I had the man with the rifle take up a position where he could see the whole deck area of the boat and gave him instructions to hold his position and to only take a shot in the event wherein a gun battle ensued. He said he understood, and the other two men with shotguns accompanied me down the float to the vessel. All three of us were armed with shotguns, and I was also carrying my .357 Smith and Wesson revolver in a holster, which was visible on my hip.

As we walked down the float to the vessel, I felt very vulnerable, having nowhere to hide if things did go bad. It was a feeling I'd never experienced before. I was a pretty big boy, and those pilings were not a lot of cover in the event of any shots being fired.

Upon our reaching the vessel, I identified myself and called out, ordering all parties aboard to come out on the deck. The four men I had transported from the Seldovia Lodge came out of the cabin to the deck of the vessel. The owner started yelling at me, asking why I had come to his boat with armed men. I ask him who had shot the weapon, and he blamed the shot on us. He said a local man had come aboard and hit him in the face with no provocation, and now the police were harassing him and he hadn't done anything. I informed the man he had a choice to make. He could leave the boat harbor, with his boat and crew, or he could go to jail. I told him he could anchor in Seldovia Bay or he could tie off to the barge that was moored in the Bay, to wait out the weather. Reluctantly he said he and his crew would leave. He directed one of the men to start the engine. A short time after the engine was running, he told the deckhands to untie the vessel.

NOTE: *A trained police officer would never have allowed anyone who has been drinking and possibly in an intoxicated state, to operate a boat or any other motor vehicle, but I was not a trained officer and I was trying to see to the safety of everyone involved. The possible alcohol impairment did not even cross my mind.*

The owner pulled away from the float and he immediately got on the radio and called the Diamond Ridge marine operator and asked that they connect him with the Alaska State Troopers.

NOTE: The Diamond Ridge marine operator assists mariners by patching radio conversations from the VHF radio into the telephone system, making it possible for a mariner to call a telephone number when they were offshore where no telephones were available.

As soon as the troopers came on the line, the owner told them he needed assistance in Seldovia. He told them he was being run out of town and they were being shot at. The trooper told him to get in touch with Seldovia Police Department, and the owner told them that it was the police who were running them out of town and shooting at them. Since the call was over the radio, everyone could hear both sides of the conversation, and we just shook our heads in disbelief that he was telling the troopers he was being shot at. I couldn't call the troopers because of the telephones being out all over town, so I can only imagine what they were thinking.

While he was talking to the troopers, he continued to maneuver the boat. Instead of backing out and swinging the bow of the boat toward the float, he swung the bow of the boat away from the float, toward the beach. He wound up going hard aground and he couldn't back off of the beach. He was now stuck aground with a deep "V" hulled vessel, and the tide was going out. It would not be long before his boat started to list and then it would roll over when the water went out from under it due to the deep "V" configuration of the boat's hull. I heard the owner tell the troopers he had to go because he was aground. He told them he'd call them back later.

Knowing the boat would roll over after the tide went out, I contacted Jim Hopkins, a friend of mine who owned a local construction company. I asked if he would bring his D-7 Caterpillar, with a winch, down to the harbor so we could hold a boat in place throughout the tide. This would ensure it would not rollover. Jim responded and hauled the D-7 Caterpillar down to the harbor with his lowboy and tractor. The winch line was pulled out and, with the assistance of a skiff, the line was taken aboard the boat. I told them to secure the cable to something solid that we could pull on to hold the boat in place and keep it from rolling over. After they secured the line, they gave a signal for Jim to pick up on it. When he tightened the winch line, the capstan, that they had secured it to, was pulled off the deck and was left hanging over the starboard side of the vessel, held only by its hydraulic lines. The mast was what they should have secured the winch line to. It went through the deck of the boat to the keel, where it was secured with through bolts. I was surprised that anyone would tie off to a deck winch that was only bolted to the deck of the boat.

After the capstan was pulled off the deck of the boat, I asked another boat owner if he would go alongside and tie his vessel to the grounded boat, to ensure the boat did not lay over. The skipper said he would go alongside and would secure his boat to it and would stay through the tide, holding it up. He said as soon as they floated again, he would assist the boat and see that it was secured to the float.

I contacted the owner of the grounded vessel and told him I didn't want any further problems in Seldovia and, due to all the problems with his boat, he didn't have to leave the harbor after his boat floated. He didn't say anything, but I knew he'd heard me. I also told him I'd overheard his conversation with the troopers and that I didn't appreciate his lies. That was when he informed me that the skipper of his vessel was not even aboard and that we'd ordered him to leave town without his skipper on the boat. He said all of this was the police department's fault. This was the first time I was told that the owner was not the skipper of the vessel. It turned out a local Seldovia resident had been hired to run the boat. Before I left the scene, the skipper of the boat did show up, highly intoxicated, and he and the owner got into a huge argument. I left before I had to get involved. I decided I'd let them work it out.

The boat that went alongside the grounded vessel was able to keep it upright and was successful in getting the damaged vessel back alongside the float where it was secured. I went down to the boat the next morning and asked the owner if I could come aboard. He said I could and I asked what the damage to the boat consisted of. He told me he really didn't know but hoped it was only to the capstan winch. While

I was on board, I observed a double-barrel 20-gauge shotgun lying on the deck between the planks of the crab rack. I picked it up and asked who owned the gun. No one on board would admit ownership, so I told the crew I'd take the gun as evidence of the shot that was fired if no one was going to claim it. Still no one claimed the shotgun, so I took it and logged it into evidence and secured it in the evidence room at the police department. It was two years later that the owner of the gun came by the PD and claimed the weapon. I released it to him, knowing he wouldn't know anything about the gun if he wasn't the owner.

Upon leaving the boat harbor, I drove to the Seldovia Lodge where I contacted the owner and talked to him about the problems that had occurred. He denied being at the Lodge when the fracas took place, and said he didn't know anything about the 4-5-6 game. I told him I'd heard rumors that he allowed gambling in his establishment quite often and I told him if it continued, I would be in touch with the Alcohol Beverage Control Board. I told him his liquor license could be in jeopardy if this continued. He said he'd do what he could to discourage gambling in the bar. I told him to have his bartenders stop it when it starts, and he said he would.

Three or four months had gone by following the incident when, one morning, I was called to the city manager's office. Upon arrival, I was told that the owner of the boat that was damaged had filed a lawsuit in the Kenai District Court House, naming the city of Seldovia and me, personally, for the damages alleged to have occurred in the incident stemming from the actions I'd taken in the Seldovia Boat Harbor when the boat had gone aground. I was told we were being sued for more than $1,000,000.00. I had never been named in a lawsuit before and I became somewhat concerned. I felt, given the circumstances, I would be found to be justified in how I had handled the matter.

Approximately a week later, I was given a deposition, and I was completely honest in what I had done and what decisions I'd made and why I had made them. Following the deposition, I still felt I could win the case but, when I read the boat owner's deposition, I found it was full of lies. I started wondering who the court would believe, given the untruths by the boat owner. I asked the city attorney if he thought we had a problem, and he said civil suits were difficult to read, but it all depended on what the judge would believe. Now I was worried. It was another three weeks before the matter came up again, and I was again called to the city office. I was ushered into the city manager's office by the city clerk/treasurer and, upon entry, I found the city attorney to be present. The attorney told me he had taken the case to a judge who was a friend of his, and he had asked him his opinion. The judge told him, after reading the case, he would find in favor of the boat owner and he would order the city to pay dearly. He said he would further find the chief of police punitively liable, and I would be facing a large personal fine. He said what I had done bordered on negligence, and I could have gotten someone killed by my actions.

You could have knocked me over with a feather. I felt I had acted in good faith and that I'd thought everything through. The problem existed when I made the decision to put an intoxicated man in control of a motor vehicle and, in doing so, I had endangered numerous lives. I accepted the fact that I'd made a huge error and I learned a very important lesson through the experience. The lesson would last for the rest of my career, and it was the last time I was ever named in a lawsuit. I'm not saying I didn't make mistakes in the future, but they weren't of that magnitude. The lawsuit was settled through negotiations, which are very common, and the city wound up paying the boat owner $38,000.

Years later, the boat owner died in a fire in Soldotna, and three Alaska state troopers called me, asking where I was on the day of the fire. The three troopers who called were good friends of mine and thought they were being funny at the time. I personally didn't find a lot of humor in it. (Case Closed Through a Cash Settlement)

4-5-6 Game #2

It was only a couple months after the incident with the boat that I received a call regarding another 4-5-6 dice game going on at the Seldovia Lodge. The caller, who wished to remain anonymous, said a 4-5-6 game was taking place on the pool table at the Seldovia Lodge and there were 15–20 people involved. The caller said he had not seen so much money in one place for a long time.

It was the height of king crab fishing season, and the highline fishermen were throwing money around like it would last forever. Everyone was making good money and didn't mind spending it on alcohol and gambling. With all the money in Seldovia, many problems involving alcohol were occurring.

I responded to the Seldovia Lodge but I didn't know how I was going to deal with this situation when I arrived. I thought to myself that I would just go there and let the chips fall where they may. After all, I had got a report of an illegal activity, and I had to check it out. Whatever happened, happened. I had learned to be straightforward in my dealings with people, and I wasn't about to back away, or change my strategy now. I walked into the hallway of the Seldovia Lodge. The hallway led to the bar and restaurant area, but just prior to entering the bar area was a pool room located on the right. When I looked into the pool room, I observed a group of people completely surrounding a pool table. Everyone was hooting and hollering, and the man with the dice was shaking them in his right hand and getting ready to roll them. He was telling everyone to place their bets. I walked up behind him, unseen by anyone. Everyone was so engrossed in the game that they didn't even notice me until I grabbed the man's right arm. This got everyone's attention. The place got quiet, and I told the crowd that they were very lucky people in that I had to take a leak, but I told them when I came out of the bathroom I would be dealing with this problem, if it still existed. I let the man's arm go and I walked into the men's room.

I got a glimpse of all the money on the pool table and I have no doubt there were a couple thousand dollars there, at a minimum. I have never seen that much money in any game since that evening.

After a few minutes, I walked back out of the bathroom and, to my relief, there was no one at the pool table, and all the money had been removed. I walked into the bar area and called the bartender over. I ask if the owner was there, and he said the owner was out of town and wouldn't be back for a few days. I told the bartender that he was responsible for the actions and activities that took place on licensed premises and I would be talking to his boss when he returned about the 4-5-6 game the bartender had allowed to take place. I also told him we'd had major problems in the past due to a 4-5-6 game that had been held here at the Lodge. I informed him it was a crime and that I would be making rounds all night, adding that I would be conducting an arrest if I found another game going on there. I informed him that he could do jail time, that the bar could lose its liquor license, and he now would be making the decisions about what was to happen next. I told him I was holding him personally responsible for any illegal games held here while his boss was out of town.

I was so relieved when I walked out the door of the Seldovia Lodge that evening. I literally do not know how I would have reacted had they still been playing when I came out of the bathroom. I don't know if they stopped out of fear of the consequences or out of respect for me. They had to know I would take some legal action if they didn't stop the activity. Either way, I was happy with the results. (Case Closed by Investigation)

Sexual Assault and Sexual Abuse of a Minor

On March 3, 1980, at approximately 2300 hours, I received a call from a distraught mother who reported her daughter, and her daughter's friend, who was staying the night, had not come home, and it was nearing midnight. She said they had told her they would be home by 2230 hours. Both girls were sixteen years of age and they should have been home, she said. I asked her where they said they were going, and she said they were supposed to be just walking around town. I told the lady I would check around but that I'd been out patrolling for a couple hours and hadn't seen them on the streets. I again took to the streets in an attempt to locate the two girls. I drove around town but didn't see them anywhere. I stopped a couple teenage boys and asked if they had seen the girls, and both said they had seen them earlier but not for a couple hours. I really had no idea where to look, so I went back to the complainant's home and asked her to call a couple of her daughter's friends and see if they knew where the girls might be. She called three different friends of her daughter's, but no one had any information regarding the two girls' whereabouts. I was about to leave the residence when the lady's daughter arrived home, but she was alone. She said she had been riding around town with a local teenager but said she didn't know where her friend had gone. The friend had left her around 2200 hours, when she'd hooked up with another teenage girl. She said the two girls left and said they were going walking around town.

After questioning the lady's daughter, I left the residence and drove around town hoping I could find the other girl. I stopped two different vehicles, being driven around by older teenagers, and asked if they had seen the girl, but no one seemed to know where she had gone. At 0030 hours, I checked back with the complainant to see if the girl had come home, and she said she hadn't and that she was getting very concerned. She said she had called the girl's parents and had informed them that the girl had not returned home with her daughter, and she said the girl's parents were quite upset to hear this. They had left directions for the complainant to call them when, and if, the girl did show up. I told the complainant to call me as well because I had exhausted all my leads and didn't know where to even look. I took another pass around town and then went home, arriving home shortly after 0100 hours.

The following morning, around 0830 hours, I received a call from the complainant reporting that her daughter's friend had arrived at their home around 0230 hours and that she was intoxicated when she came home. The complainant told me she had called the girl's parents and informed them about the condition of their daughter. She said she'd put her to bed and the girl was sleeping now. She further told me that she hadn't called me because she didn't really want to disturb me and she didn't feel there was much I could do until the girl sobered up. I told the complainant to let her sleep it off and that I would be contacting her later in the day. Shortly after noon, I drove over to the complainant's residence to talk to the girl, but she had already left and had gone to her own residence. The complainant said she had tried to get some information, but the girl was not forthcoming, and she didn't know where she had been or who had given her the alcohol. I thanked the complainant and drove over to the girl's home. Upon arrival, I knocked on the door, and the girl's mother answered. I asked if her daughter was home, and she said she was and further, that she had been expecting me.

The daughter came out of her room, and the three of us sat down at the kitchen table. The girl's father was not home at the time, and I asked her mother if she had any problem with my questioning her daughter with her present. She said she did not. I asked her daughter where she had been the night before. She first told me she was just walking around, but I told her I'd already talked with the friend she was supposed to spend the night with, and I knew she'd left her before 2300 hours, and had gone with another girl. I also told her I knew she'd consumed alcohol. After telling her I knew she'd been drinking, she told me she and her friend had gone to a house where two guys were staying and they'd had the beer. She said a case of Olympia beer was on the table when they went inside. She said the two men were twenty-one and twenty-two years of age, and she told me their names. I was well acquainted with both the men and knew them to be old enough to visit bars. She said she and her friend were walking by the two men's homes when they were invited inside. They were offered beer by the 22-year-old. I asked how much alcohol she had consumed, and she said probably four or five beers. When asked, she said her friend had consumed about the same amount. I inquired if her friend was intoxicated, and she said probably, because she drank about the same amount as she had.

I then asked if anything sexual had taken place, and the girl quickly said no, but she looked down when answering, which indicated to me there was more to the story than she was telling. She said they had made out, kissed, but that was as far as the two girls would let it go. The guys wanted to go further but did not push it, she said. Upon further questioning regarding any sexual activity, the girl started to cry. After a few minutes, she told her mother and I that the 22-year-old had coaxed her into a bedroom and had started feeling her breasts outside her clothing; she had told him to stop, but he wouldn't take no for an answer. She said he forced himself on her, pulling her pants and panties down and then sexually assaulted her. I asked if her friend had been sexually assaulted as well, and she stated she didn't think so but really didn't know. Her friend had left the residence before she had.

Upon the girl's allegation of being sexually assaulted, I felt the need to call the Alaska State Troopers, since I'd never investigated anything of this nature and really didn't know what all would be needed. I also wanted to have enough information regarding the other girl's involvement before calling the Alaska State Troopers for assistance.

I told the girl's mother that I was going to get some assistance in the investigation because I hadn't investigated a crime of this nature and I really didn't want to mess it up. She said she understood, and I told her I would be back to continue the investigation after I got some advice from the Alaska State Troopers. I also told her that if her daughter hadn't taken a shower, not to allow her to take one yet and not to allow her to wash up. She assured that me she would see to it.

I left the girl's residence and went to the residence of the friend who had been with her at the home of the two men. Upon arriving at the girl's residence, I was greeted by her father and her mother. I told them I was conducting an investigation into some underage drinking and some sexual allegations that were made, and I needed to talk to their daughter. They invited me in and called their daughter, who came out of her room. I told her what I was there for, and the four of us sat down at the kitchen table where I questioned the 16-year-old. I told her I'd talked to the friend she'd been with the night before, and that she should be completely honest with me because I already had a lot of information about what had happened. On questioning her, she admitted to having a couple beers; she said the 21-year-old had made advances, but she'd made him stop. He had felt her breasts on the outside of her clothing and had attempted to reach under her blouse, but she pushed him away. He then put his hand down her pants and felt of her genital area, but she told him to stop and pushed him back. She said she was able to get away from him and run out the door. She hadn't wanted to leave her friend there alone but was afraid to stay, she said. I asked her if she knew what, if anything, had happened to her friend, and she said she did not and the last time she saw her, the friend and the 22-year-old had gone into the other room. She said she had stayed in the living room with the 21-year-old.

I thanked the girl for being honest with me, and told her and her parents I would be back to deal with this further, after I got some direction from the Alaska State Troopers. I told them I had never investigated a case of this nature and I didn't want to make any mistakes.

The parents thanked me and said they would keep their daughter home and wait for me to contact them. I left their residence and went to my office where I called the Alaska State Troopers.

Trooper Mike Dowd, of the Homer Post of the AST, answered the phone, and I went over all the information I had up to this point in my investigation with him. He told me to contact the parents of the two girls and have them accompany the girls to Homer, where they could be further interviewed, and a SART examination could be conducted. He told me to tell the girls not to shower or wash up until after the medical examination took place and that they should bag the clothes they were wearing at the time for further examination by the State Laboratory.

A Sexual Assault Response Team (SART) investigates sexual assault and sexual abuse victims. The examination is done by a team of trained medical professionals who interview and examine sexual assault/abuse victims in a hospital setting. The examinations then become evidence in any upcoming court proceedings.

Trooper Dowd told me to let the parents know that the state would be paying for their airfare to and from Homer. He also told me he would most probably be accompanying them back to Seldovia on their return trip so we could contact the two men and get their side of the story.

I terminated my call with Trooper Dowd and called both parents and conveyed what the Trooper had told me. I then made arrangements for their travel to Homer and back and relayed the information to them. I asked if they needed transportation to the airport, and they said they did not. I told them their flight was scheduled for 1500 hours and that the trooper would be meeting them when they arrived in Homer. I then called Trooper Dowd back with the information and the time they would be landing in Homer. He said he'd call when they were headed back to Seldovia following the SART examination.

At 1845 hours, I met Trooper Dowd, the victims, and their parents at the Seldovia airport. Trooper Dowd told them he would be in touch with them as the case progressed, but the girls should not have any contact with the two suspects, and should not talk about the case to any of their friends. The girls said they understood, and everyone left the airport.

Trooper Dowd told me he would like to interview the two suspects starting with the 21-year-old. I drove to the residence where the alleged assaults took place, and we found both the men there. I told the 21-year-old that we needed to talk to him at the police department and that we would provide transportation. I told the 22-year-old that we'd be back to talk to him a little later and for him to stay put.

We drove to the police department and Trooper Dowd read the 21-year-old his Miranda rights warning. He stated he understood his rights and agreed to talk to us. He signed the Waiver of Rights form, and an interview was conducted with him. After a time, he admitted to touching the one girl in the area of her breast and between her legs but said nothing happened other than that. Following the interview, Trooper Dowd placed the 21-year-old under arrest and told him he would be charged with "Sexual Abuse of a Minor" and would be transported to Homer Jail. The trooper asked if I would watch the 21-year-old while he interviewed the 22-year-old and, since we had no jail facility, I told the trooper I would sit with him in the other room. The trooper then left, to go pick up the 22-year-old. He brought him to the police department for the interview. I kept the 21-year-old in the other room, out of sight or earshot of the trooper and the 22-year-old. After approximately thirty minutes, the trooper told me the interview was over, and the 22-year-old was under arrest for "Sexual Assault in the 1st Degree." He asked that I make arrangements for an airplane to take him and the prisoners to Homer. I called Cook Inlet Aviation, and a flight was scheduled for 2045 hours. I transported Trooper Dowd and the two young men to the airport, where they boarded the airplane on their way to Homer Jail.

At the arraignment, the 21-year-old was held on a $5,000 bond, while the 22-year-old was held on a $10,000 bond and a third-party custodian. He would have to have someone approved by the court who would swear to keep the 22-year-old in sight or sound, 24 hours a day, seven days a week, if he was able to make bail.

A Grand Jury was called, and indictments were handed down for both men. The 21-year-old was charged with "Sexual Abuse of a Minor" and the 22-year-old was charged with "Sexual Assault of a Minor in the 1st Degree." The 21-year-old pled "No Contest" at his court hearing, and he was found guilty of "Sexual Abuse of a Minor." He was sentenced to 270 days in jail with a $1000 fine. Upon release from jail, he would be on probation for five years. He was not to have any contact with juveniles under eighteen years of age, he was not to consume any alcohol, and he could have no weapons. He also had to stay in monthly contact with his probation officer.

The 22-year-old pled Not Guilty, and a date was set for a jury trial. He was held on the $10,000 bond, and a third-party custodian was ordered.

Within three months a "Change of Plea" hearing was held, and the 22-year-old changed his plea from "Not Guilty to "No Contest." He was adjudicated guilty of "Sexual Assault in the 1st Degree" and was sentenced to four years in jail with two years suspended. He would be given credit for time served, and when he got out of jail, he was to have no contact with juveniles under the age of eighteen years of age. He would be on probation for five years and was directed to consume no alcohol, have no firearms, and to abide by the general conditions set down by the court, which included no contact with convicted felons, submit to a search of his home, vehicle or person when directed to do so by his probation officer, to check in monthly with his probation officer, and to obey all laws and ordinances.

Both men, the 21-year-old and the 22-year-old, chose not to return to Seldovia and both took up residence with relatives in Anchorage.

This was my first case involving sexual assault and/or sexual abuse of a minor, and I learned a great deal from the experience. My gratitude and heartfelt thanks go out to trooper Mike Dowd for sharing his expertise and knowledge with me. Another Alaska state trooper who helped me along the path of my career. I hold the Alaska state troopers in high esteem. I was very happy when "Justice Was Served" for the two victims in this case. (Case Closed by Arrest)

A New Badge in Town

I was notified of a new program that was available through the state in the form of a grant. It was called the CETA program; eligible municipalities could hire new employees, and the state would help the municipality pay the costs for the employee for three years. The state would pick up three-fourth of the cost of the employee for the first year, half of the cost for the employee in the second year and one-fourth of the cost in the third year. For the fourth year, the city agreed to fund the position in full. I asked the city manager for permission to apply for the grant, and he took it before the city council. The council gave me a green light, and I filled out the grant application forms. It took a couple months, but I did receive an affirmative response, opening the door for me to hire a patrol officer. It was made very clear by the state that the employee's wages, his benefits, and a progress report would all have to be submitted quarterly while the employee was working. Failure to do so would result in the grant being canceled. The city office personnel would take care of seeing to the report, but I would need to give them an evaluation of the employee every three months. I would become a supervisor and I barely knew how to do the job myself. I felt somewhat intimidated, to say the least.

The city posted the position of a patrol officer and put it in the *Homer News* as well as the *Anchorage Times*. Alfred Bond, a local young man, had shown an interest in becoming a police officer, so I called him and told him, if he was still interested in being a cop, he should go to the city office and apply in person for the position. I told him he would have to fill out an employment form, and a background check would have to be done, but I felt he had a very good chance of being hired, in that he was a local resident. Mr. Bond did as I requested and in approximately six weeks, he was hired as the first patrol officer in the Seldovia Police Department. Other more qualified applicants were not considered due to a local man applying for the position.

Since I was now a supervisor, and, having never had any formal training in law enforcement myself, and literally learning as I went along, I felt like the blind leading the blind. Officer Bond asked me a lot of questions and those I knew the answer to, I would answer, but for the questions I didn't know the answers to, I would call on the troopers for assistance. Officer Bond and I developed a great working relationship and we both learned a lot while we were working together. Officer Bond would work for a year and a half before leaving the position. He covered the night shift while I worked days. Officer Bond's shift gave him Monday and Tuesday off, with him covering the weekends. I always monitored my radio and stayed ready to respond to any assistance he may have needed, which actually did happen quite often.

Officer Bond and I stayed very busy. Many investigations and actions were taken by the Seldovia Police Department, resulting from the many incidents and cases that occurred in 1980. The cases that were investigated consisted of three theft cases, three reports of shooting within the city limits, one impoundment of an illegally parked forty van, one death investigation, one shoplifting report, five reports of criminal mischief, three burglaries of residences, one felony theft, three fire reports, one report of reckless endangerment, one weapons misconduct investigation, three assaults on a person, two investigations for furnishing liquor to minors, three minors consuming alcohol, one report of disorderly conduct, two felony assaults and four motor vehicle accidents. Along with the investigations, we were continuously working traffic, doing bar checks, and responding to other public requests, which included EMT calls, medivacs, animal control reports, overdue juveniles, and a myriad other requests for assistance. It would be impossible to elaborate on all the calls and investigations we dealt with so I am attempting to be more specific on the more interesting cases that I feel the reader would enjoy reading. I was still an untrained officer and I was amazed at the number of calls that came into the police department in our small town.

MISCONDUCT INVOLVING WEAPONS
IN THE SECOND DEGREE

I t was Saturday, August 14, 1980, and even though I was on call, I was hoping for a quiet night, which I hoped would continue throughout Sunday. A friend, Rob Painter, his wife Jane, and their two children had traveled from Anchorage to spend the weekend with Ann and I and our daughter Donica. Rob and I had worked together for a couple years when we were employed by a diving company on the waterfront in Anchorage. Rob was a mechanic and all-around good hand, and I ran their tug boats, diving boats, and heavy equipment, as well as worked in their construction yard.

Ann, Donica, and I had been busy showing our guests around the Seldovia area and we were a little late in fixing dinner. The wives were preparing the salads and other dishes while our kids were busy entertaining one another. Rob and I had a fire going and were boiling water, ready to cook up some fresh king crab. We were looking forward to enjoying a fresh seafood dinner with all the trimmings.

It was around 2110 hours, and Rob and I were reminiscing about old times when the police phone rang. I excused myself and answered the call. The Seldovia Lodge's bartender reported that a fight had occurred just minutes before between four cannery workers. She told me they had gotten into a scuffle inside the bar and had been ushered outside, where the fight escalated. She said the fight was between two Caucasians and a Vietnamese and a Filipino. The Vietnamese man and the Filipino had left the area, threatening to get a shotgun and come back and even the score. The bartender insisted I respond immediately as she did not know how long it would be before the Vietnamese and Filipino returned. She said she was convinced they were serious about going after a shotgun.

I apologized to Rob and Jane and told them I had a call I had to go on, but would hopefully be able to handle it quickly and be back for dinner. I told them not to hold dinner if I wasn't back but I was hoping this wouldn't take long. I really didn't know what I was going into.

I geared up and responded to the Seldovia Lodge where I found the two Caucasian cannery workers waiting for me outside the bar. One of the two had gone to his room and had gotten his .380 Titan automatic pistol after the Vietnamese man had opened his coat, revealing a pair of nunchucks. The cannery worker told me he had armed himself for self-protection. I took the weapon from him and unloaded it. I told the two that they were not going to turn this into an all-out gun battle and that the man could pick up his weapon at the police department on Monday.

The two men said they were inside the bar when the Vietnamese and Filipino came in and started the problem. They said there had been a verbal altercation at the cannery earlier in the day between the four of them, but it was only a lot of yelling at that time. Both said they were surprised to see it escalate to this point. When they were accosted by the two Asians inside the bar, the verbal assault nearly led to punches. This resulted in the bartender telling all of them to take it outside. They said the arguing continued outside the bar and when the nunchucks were seen, the cannery worker said he went for his pistol. When he showed the two Asians the pistol, they ran to their vehicle. The Vietnamese man yelled out the threats regarding them going after a shotgun. The cannery worker with the pistol told me he never pointed the weapon at the two Asians but he did show it to them, hoping to defuse the situation. I ordered the two to get inside the bar and to stay there; under no circumstances were they to come outside until this matter was handled. I also told them to tell the bartender to keep everyone else inside the bar until this was over.

I made sure the cannery workers and the other bar patrons would be safe. Officer Bond was out of town and not available at the time, so I called my wife on the radio and requested she contact Gerry Willard, a councilman and a good friend, and tell him I needed assistance at the Seldovia Lodge and, further, that he was to bring a shotgun. Due to the heat of the moment, I never really considered how that call must have impacted my wife and my guests. At that time during my career, I had no other options when calling for assistance. My only means of communication was by radio. I was later told by my wife that quite a discussion had followed between her and my guests after I made that radio call. I can only imagine what they must have thought at the time.

I knew I had to take whatever steps necessary to ensure the safety of everyone inside the bar. I had to see to it, at any cost, that the Filipino and the Vietnamese did not return and enter the Seldovia Lodge with a weapon. The bar was full of patrons, and if a shotgun, or any weapon for that matter, was discharged inside, many people could have been severely injured, if not killed.

After making sure everyone was inside the lodge, I took up a position between two vehicles just to the west of the steps leading up to the entry door of the bar. Anyone entering the lodge could only gain access by way of those steps. On my left was a window van, with a four-door sedan parked to my right. I was waiting approximately three or four minutes when I observed a black Cadillac quickly enter the parking area, just west of the van, and come to a sliding stop. I knew the Cadillac belonged to the Vietnamese cannery worker. I was surprised no one immediately exited the vehicle. It was at least another minute or so before the passenger door was thrown open, and the Vietnamese man exited, holding a shotgun high over his head. With no hesitation, he started running toward the steps leading up to the Seldovia Lodge's main entrance. It was dark, but a street light, located ahead and to the east of the sedan, illuminated the area, and I could easily see everything that was taking place. I had un-holstered my 357 Smith & Wesson revolver when the Vietnamese man exited the vehicle and, when he ran across in front of me, I drew down on him and yelled, "Police officer, drop the weapon." The man immediately stopped running and swung his head in my direction in an effort to see where I was positioned. I again ordered him to drop the weapon. He was now looking at me, and the shotgun was still being held above his head with the barrel pointed away from me.

I've been told on a number of occasions, by other police officers, that when you're dealing with this type of high-stress situation, time often seems to go into slow motion. Your thought patterns speed up and you are able to make a number of decisions in a fraction of the time it would normally take. I found this to be true in this instance. As I held my weapon on him at center mass, I mentally took in the fact that the barrel of the shotgun was pointing away from me and was not a threat to me at this time. I literally told myself, if the weapon was swung around in my direction, I was going to shoot this man. The Vietnamese man must have detected something in my demeanor that convinced him he was about to die because, after only a few seconds, he dropped the weapon to the ground. Prior to his dropping the weapon, I could see the indecision in his eyes. I felt he was gauging his chances of shooting me before I could shoot him. Luckily, for both of us, he made the right decision.

Immediately after he dropped the shotgun, I ordered him face down on the ground. He dropped to his knees and then took a prone position face down without any hesitation, and I then placed him in handcuffs. I told him to remain in that position and not to move. Upon patting him down for additional weapons I found the nunchucks inside his coat, tucked into his waistband. I took the nunchucks from his waistband and then picked up the shotgun. It was a 20-gauge, Remington pump, with a visibly modified choke. The buttstock had been sawed off, making a pistol-type grip. When I hit the release and pumped the action, a 20-gauge, 8-shot, shotgun shell ejected from the chamber. The plug had been taken out of the weapon, and I extracted another four rounds from the magazine. I picked up the extracted shells and directed the Vietnamese man to get up. I walked him to my patrol vehicle. I stored the nunchucks, the shotgun, and the shells in the rear of the patrol vehicle and then walked the suspect to the passenger door. As I was loading him into the police vehicle, he said to me, "Kill me, or I'll come back and kill you and your family." I told him to knock it off, that nobody was going to kill anyone. He then said, "You kill me or I kill myself." He then stuck his tongue out between his teeth and started biting down on it. As I put the seat belt on him, I told him, "Go ahead, you're only simplifying my paperwork." You would have thought I had given him a sedative. He calmed down immediately and stopped biting his tongue. He must have thought I really didn't care either way and, further, that he wasn't impressing me with his antics.

I had never had any formal police training up to this point in my career and I didn't know that it is policy, in almost all police departments, to never fully cock a double-action revolver in any instance, due to the possibility of an accidental discharge. I had cocked the hammer on my weapon when I took it out of its holster upon the Vietnamese man exiting the vehicle. I only took the hammer off its fully cocked position after the man had dropped the shotgun. Later, at the AST Police Academy, I learned to always shoot double action so as not to create an unnecessary hazard.

As I loaded the man into the patrol vehicle, Gerry Willard drove up in his van. He jumped out and came over to the patrol vehicle carrying a shotgun and asked me what was going on. I told him his timing really did stink but to meet me at the police department and I'd fill him in. I then transported my prisoner to my office at City Hall.

I escorted the Vietnamese man into my office and, after transferring his handcuffs from his back to in front of him, I sat him down in a chair facing my desk. I then called the Seldovia Lodge and told the bartender that the threat had been eliminated and her patrons were again free to come and go as they pleased.

I explained to Mr. Willard what had taken place up until this point. I told him I needed to start the paperwork and get this information on the Vietnamese. As Mr. Willard stood by, I asked the man a series of questions. He was not forthcoming, and I was having a great deal of difficulty getting any information from him at all.

I continued my efforts until approximately one half hours later, when the police telephone rang. I answered the phone, and the bartender at the Knight Spot Bar on Main Street was demanding I respond to the bar immediately. He said a Filipino man was inside the bar swinging two large knives around and that he was angry, and the bartender was afraid someone was going to be killed or hurt badly if the man wasn't stopped.

Since we didn't have a jail or holding facility, I asked Mr. Willard if he would watch the prisoner so I could check out a weapons complaint report at the Knight Spot Bar. He said he would, and I left the office, responding code 2 to the bar. Upon arrival, I approached the entry door with caution. The barroom itself opened into the bar area, 90 degrees to the right, immediately after entry.

As I approached the closed door from outside, I unholstered the 357 Smith & Wesson for the second time that day. I pushed the door open with my right foot and I was shocked to see the Filipino man standing directly in front of the door. He was holding two blades in his hands, one being a large hunting knife and the other being a sword with a blade approximately two and a half feet in length. Both weapons were being held with their blades pointing upward. I brought my pistol to center mass on the man's chest and ordered him to drop the weapons. He didn't drop them but did lower them, crossing them in front of him. Fearing he would attempt to use one or both of the blades, I kicked out with my left foot, hitting the knives, knocking both weapons out of his hands. Before landing on the floor, the Filipino sustained a cut from one of the blades to the inside of the second finger of his right hand while I received a small cut on the back of my right hand. As soon as the knives hit the floor, I hit the Filipino in the chest with the heel of my left hand, sending him reeling back into a cigarette machine located directly behind him. I quickly holstered my weapon and grabbed the man as he starting to collapse to the floor. I lifted him up and shoved him face-first into the wall, holding him against the wall with my right hand in the middle of his back. I reached for my second set of handcuffs to handcuff him when I noticed I was holding him so firmly against the wall that both his feet were approximately six inches off the floor. I had such an adrenaline rush that I hadn't realized the amount of force I was applying. The Filipino was a very small man, approximately five feet four tall and could not have weighed more than 110 pounds, soaking wet. After easing the pressure off on his back, letting him slide down to where his feet were touching the floor, I placed him in handcuffs. As I was patting him down for more weapons, he told me he just wanted to go to jail with his friend. I replied, "Well you made it dude," and I then picked up the knife and the sword and opened the door to take him out. It was then that I noticed the cigarette machine was leaning back against the wall, supported by only two of its four legs. I again realized I had used considerably more force than I had intended when I had hit the man in the chest in an effort to disarm him. The impact, when he hit the cigarette machine, tipped it back against the wall.

It was at that time when I actually began to note the other patrons in the bar, other than the man with a sword and a knife. I had been dealing with a dangerous situation and was focused only on that but I definitely learned the true meaning of "*Tunnel Vision.*" The bar was full of people, with hardly any empty seats, and I had been oblivious to all of it. I was thinking of how this could have all gone very wrong if the Filipino'd had a friend with him inside the bar at the time. Oh well, I thought, you take 'em where you can get 'em. When I exited the bar with my prisoner, I was given a very loud round of applause.

I transported the Filipino to the police department where Mr. Willard was guarding his friend. I transferred his handcuffs to the front, and found his finger to be bleeding and in need of attention. I asked Mr. Willard to get the first aid kit out of the other room so we could put a bandage on it. The Vietnamese man told the Filipino not to let us touch him and that he would fix the man's finger. The Vietnamese man then plucked a hair from his own head and, holding each end, he pushed it down into the sliced wound on the Filipino's finger. The blood immediately stopped flowing. I had never witnessed anything like that in my life. When I later talked to our local doctor about it, I was told he would be very surprised if the Filipino didn't wind up with a very bad staph infection. The doctor said he'd heard of tying hair together to close a scalp wound but had never heard of a hair being used to stop the bleeding of a slice type wound. He did say the Vietnamese man most probably had seen a lot of war in his lifetime, and that many different methods, unknown to us, were used to deal with injuries sustained on the battlefield in those Asian countries.

Because we didn't have a holding facility, I had to make arrangements to transport the two prisoners to Homer. Seldovia has a dirt airfield, which is not lit, but the local air taxi owner/operator was very familiar with the terrain and often had to take medivacs into Homer during the nighttime hours. I called Bob Gruber, owner/operator of Cook Inlet Aviation, and told him I needed to transport two prisoners to the Homer Jail. He said he could be ready within the hour and he would meet me at the airport.

I had gotten all the personal information I could get from my two disgruntled inmates and I made ready to transport them to the airport. I called the Homer Police Department and explained the situation to them and told them I was about ready to transport. They said they would meet the airplane at the Homer Airport and relieve me of the prisoners. I told them I hadn't been able to get too much information on the two but would have more after I contacted their employer.

After the arrangements were made to transport the two prisoners, I called my wife and told her what had gone on and what I still had to deal with. It was now 2340 hours, and I still had to take a trip to Homer and back. Ann said they'd had a great dinner and everyone was disappointed I couldn't be there. I told her I'd be home after I got back from Homer, if nothing else came up to keep me working. I told her not to wait up for me because I still had a couple hours of work before I could even think about coming home. She told me to be careful and said she'd see me when I did get home.

Mr. Willard and I readied the prisoners for transport, putting them both in transport belts, which kept them from lifting their hands above their waists. This prevented any aggressive acts by either of them while being transported. After loading them into the patrol vehicle, I transported them to the airport, where Bob Gruber already had the airplane running, warming it up for the flight. The two men were loaded into the middle seat with me in the co-pilot's seat and Mr. Gruber, of course, in the left front seat. It was a fifteen-minute flight to Homer, and an HPD jail guard officer was waiting for us to transport the two men to Homer jail. I turned over the prisoners; the guard replaced my transport belts and handcuffs with his, and I gave him the paperwork I had on both prisoners with the limited information I had obtained. He loaded both men into his van and left the airport. Mr. Gruber and I re-boarded the aircraft and, in another fifteen minutes, we were again on the ground at the Seldovia Airport. I found it somewhat terrifying to be landing in an unlit airport in total darkness, but Mr. Gruber had done it on so many previous occasions, it appeared to be no challenge at all for him. He waited until he was on final approach before turning on his landing lights and I was shocked to see us as close to the end of the airstrip as we were. I gained a lot of respect for Bob Gruber's abilities that night. That was the first night flight I'd had to take to deliver prisoners to Homer Jail and I found it to be rather exhilarating. I would take many more of these types of flights during my career.

When we were taxiing to the Cook Inlet Aviation hangar, I observed Gerry Willard waiting for us. He told me he was glad I was back home. He informed me that a number of cars were riding around the streets of Seldovia with armed citizens. Rumors had spread that the Filipino and Vietnamese cannery workers had made threats to shoot up the town and that the police had arrested two of them and had transported them to Homer Jail. Since they felt they had no police protection, with both Officer Bond and me out of town, they were taking steps to protect themselves and keeping an eye on the Asian population that worked at the cannery. I immediately left the airport in my police vehicle and started stopping vehicles and warning them against any violence. I told them no threat existed any longer and to go home, to unload their weapons and not create additional problems by overreacting. I told those who were somewhat argumentative that I wasn't opposed to transporting more prisoners to Homer during the night, if the need were to arise. That seemed to defuse the situation and within an hour, everyone was off the streets.

I arrived home around 0220 hours that night and went straight to bed. I lay there wide awake, trying to figure out how I was going to write this case up and what I was going to recommend for charges against the two men. After a time, I finally did fall asleep.

The next morning, Ann and Jane cooked breakfast and I actually got to visit with my guests prior to them flying out at 1500 hours that afternoon. That was the last time the Painters ever came to visit us in Seldovia, and I fear they got a very bad impression of our town. I did tell them this was a very unusual incident, and Seldovia, for the most part, was a very friendly, quiet and safe place to live. I informed them that usually guns did not come into play when resolving disputes but, on this occasion, that was not the case. I don't think they were convinced, even though I joked with them that this was the reason I got the big bucks. If only that were true. I felt grossly underpaid following this incident.

On Monday morning, I contacted the district attorney (DA) and laid out a scenario of what had taken place. I suggested we charge felony assault with a deadly weapon against both suspects, and asked if it was possible to bring multiple charges since so many people were impacted by the two men's actions. The DA said he would consider it and would call me later in the day. He said, either way, an arraignment had to take place or the two had to be released or they had to be given an opportunity to make bail.

Within a couple hours, the DA did call back and told me he had considered the case and asked if I would be satisfied if the Vietnamese and the Filipino were banned from ever coming back to Seldovia. He said they would be told charges would be filed against them if they ever did return to town, for any reason. I was not pleased with the suggestion and told the DA I felt the two were very dangerous and, in my opinion, we needed to get them off the streets. I told him I feared they would seriously injure or kill someone if they weren't held responsible for their actions in this matter. I expounded on the fact that none of us knew what would have taken place if I had not been successful in stopping the Vietnamese man from entering the bar with the shotgun. The DA has the final say as to whether a case is charged or not, and I believe this DA had already made up his mind that he was going to dump the case and not prefer any charges, regardless of my feelings. In thinking about it, I later felt it was most probably only a courtesy on his part that he even asked my opinion.

To cut a long story short, the two men were given instructions not to return to Seldovia; they were told felony charges would be brought against them if they failed to obey the order. They were told to have co-workers at the cannery pack up their personal belongings and send them over to them. They were then released from custody on the orders of the DA. I don't believe anyone, other than the DA and the two Asians, were happy with this decision.

After the two were released from jail, and had gotten a co-worker to send them their personal belongings, I figured that would be the end of it. However, within a week, the two Caucasian cannery workers, who had been involved in the case, came to the police department and reported that they had been told by a co-worker that the Vietnamese man had called and said he and the Filipino were camped out at the Anchorage Airport and were waiting for the two Caucasians to leave Seldovia on their way back to the continental U.S.. They reportedly were going to kill the two of them when they came off the airplane from Homer. Both of the Caucasian men were very shaken. When asked when they were planning to leave, both said in another one to two weeks but, if the two were still waiting at the Anchorage Airport, their plans would most definitely change. I assured both men I would look into the matter and I told them to report any and all threats they were told about. I instructed them not to leave Seldovia without first checking with me. They both readily agreed and said they would contact me if and when more information was received.

Due to the threats against the two Caucasian men, I contacted the Anchorage airport police and passed on what information I had on both the Asian men. After calling and talking to an officer with the airport police, I faxed him the information I had regarding the case, as well as the limited information I had on the two men. I asked that I be called and told of any contacts with the two subjects so I could notify the two victims in Seldovia when it was safe for them to travel through the Anchorage Airport. I wanted to stay on top of this to prevent anything further from taking place.

Approximately two weeks passed, when I received a call from the airport officer at the Anchorage Airport, and was told contact had been made with the two suspects. They were found to be staying at the airport, as was the information we had received, and they were informed they had to leave. They were told no one was allowed to live on airport property. The airport officer further told me the two did not leave the airport and, approximately three days following their first contact, the Vietnamese and the Filipino got into a fight, and the Vietnamese pulled a large knife and cut the Filipino's throat. The Filipino was rushed to the hospital and had to undergo surgery but he survived. When the police were going to arrest the Vietnamese man for the assault, he attempted to cut the officers with the knife as well, but he was arrested without anyone else being injured. The officer said they had gone to the hospital to get a statement from the Filipino, and they were told the Filipino had left the hospital with plans to leave Alaska immediately after he came out of recovery. Even though it was against the doctor's orders, he did not stay around to bring charges or to testify against the Vietnamese man. The officer said the Filipino was lucky to have survived and was possibly so afraid of the Vietnamese man that he just wanted to go where he could not find him. They said, upon checking the flights, the Filipino did board an airplane to Seattle. The Vietnamese man would still be charged, the officer stated, because there were other witnesses to the assault on the Filipino. The Vietnamese man would also be charged with multiple felonies due to his attempting to cut the officers who were arresting him. The officer said the Vietnamese man should spend a lot of time in jail. I thanked the officer and complimented him on a job well done.

I contacted the two cannery workers and told them the threat no longer existed, and when they asked why, I told them the Vietnamese man had been arrested on other felony charges and the Filipino man had left the state. It was apparent they were very relieved, and they thanked me for all I'd done for them. (Case Closed by Arrest)

A Man Called Swack

In July of 1980, I was privileged to become acquainted with Captain C.E. Swackhammer of the Alaska State Troopers. Swack, as he was commonly known to his friends and his associates, was well-liked by everyone. He was very intelligent, easygoing, and quick to smile. He was a high-ranking Alaska state trooper and he was able to get things done.

Shortly after I became acquainted with Swack, he told me we needed to have lunch together. I agreed, and we went to the local restaurant, the Kachemak Kafe. At this luncheon, Swack asked me if I thought the city would be receptive to negotiating a Police Service Contract between them and the Department of Public Safety (DPS). He said the contract would require the Seldovia PD to respond to all trooper calls outside the city limits of Seldovia. He said, "With the population increasing in the outer area, there would be more and more trooper-related calls, and someone will have to respond to these calls." He said we would be involved in all aspects of public safety and law enforcement in the outlying area, including the waterways in and around Seldovia Bay. He said he could see to it that DPS puts a boat in our harbor that could be used to respond to search and rescue efforts, or for any other purpose the Seldovia Police Department deemed necessary. He also said with a contract in place, the officers of the Seldovia Police Department would be given a "Special Police Commission," giving us the same authority and power as an Alaska state trooper. He explained the Special Police Commission was vitally important so as to erase any boundary disputes that might arise concerning authority issues. In talking to him further, I was told the Alaska state troopers wanted to be as helpful to the Seldovia Police Department as they could. He said they had equipment that they could make available to the Seldovia PD, and he would personally assist us in any way he could. During our luncheon, I told Swack we should set up a meeting with the city manager, and the three of us could discuss the contract. I really thought the city would be receptive to the idea.

In June of 1980, James Hampton replaced Don Caswell as the city manager. Mr. Hampton was an intelligent man, who I felt was sincere about doing a good job for the city of Seldovia, and I really felt confident he would be in favor of a contract with DPS. I was able to set up a meeting between him, Swack, and myself for that afternoon. At the meeting, Mr. Hampton said he was very interested in a police service contract but he couldn't make a commitment without first taking it before the City Council. Swack told him he understood, and Mr. Hampton said he'd make it an agenda item for the next council meeting, which was only a week away. The manager said he'd hopefully have some good news for all of us following that meeting. He asked Swack to draw up a draft contract to give him a better understanding of what all would be expected of the police department and asked that he include a ballpark dollar figure so the council would have a better idea of what they would be agreeing to. He said he would do all he could to convince the council to consider the contract. The meeting was very positive, and we all walked away feeling good about what we had accomplished.

Long story short, we did come to an agreement on a contract, which brought a few thousand dollars into the city coffers every year. The Alaska state troopers delivered a 21' Boston Whaler, powered with a 150 hp Johnson outboard, as promised, to the Seldovia Harbor shortly after the contract was enacted. We found Swack to be a man of his word and to have a genuine interest in the Seldovia Police Department. That "Agreement for Services Contract," which we negotiated during that meeting, is still in effect today, now twenty-nine years later. Each year following its inception, the DPS continues to renew the contract and, the amount of the contract increases every few years, as well.

We also were fortunate to have Swack's input on the floorplan for a jail facility we were planning to build. Plans were to build it at the same time the fire department facility was under construction. Swack sat down with me and drew up a floorplan for the jail facility, showing me what DPS would need if we were to ever negotiate a jail contract with them. With a jail contract in place, Swack said we could hold prisoners up to ten days. This would allow locals, who were sentenced to jail time, to spend their time here in Seldovia. As it turned out, we were able to build the jail facility and we were able to get a jail contract with DPS. The downside is that the contract only lasted for a few years. During that time, we employed jail guards and fed the prisoners from the local restaurants, and DPS picked up the cost. When we lost the jail contract, due to the low numbers of prisoners housed, we still retained the service contract, wherein we still responded to all AST calls in our area. Swack was very good for the city of Seldovia. Over time, he also made two police vehicles, as well as other necessities, available to the Seldovia PD. Even though the two vehicles had been retired by DPS, they still were in much better condition than the vehicles we were driving at the time.

The Seldovia "Fuzzball"

The Seldovia Police Department was in need of supplies, which would enable us to conduct our investigations more thoroughly and more professionally, but the city did not have the funding to purchase the needed equipment. I ask Mr. Hampton, the city manager, if he would allow me to put on a winter festival with games, snow machine races, a community dinner, and a talent show, in an effort to raise money for needed supplies. I had already run the idea by Elaine Giles, the clerk/treasurer for the city, and she was on board immediately. She was very excited about the idea, and told me she would start an account for the festival and would keep track of all the money that was generated through the different activities.

In selling the idea to Mr. Hampton, I told him that I felt it would be very beneficial in relieving winter stress, the cabin fever syndrome, and would give people something to take part in. I also mentioned the economic advantages the city would experience through the hotels, restaurants, and bars. I brought up the sales tax that would be generated, and Mr. Hampton, without hesitation, signed off on the idea. The planning phase immediately started for the implementation of the festival. I called a meeting of interested parties, and a committee of volunteers was formed. We had two or three meetings, and many different ideas were discussed. In trying to come up with a catchy name for the festival, a number of ideas were suggested. They brought up names like "The Pig Festival," "The Policeman's Ball," "The Seldovia

Police Festival," and then someone mentioned "The Fuzz Ball." No more discussion regarding a name was necessary. It was unanimous. Everyone wanted it to be called "The Fuzz Ball," so it stuck, and for eight years we had a three to four-day event, which always took place in the middle of February. We had snow machine and four-wheeler races, old-time Seldovia movies, kids' games every day the event took place and, toward the end of each festival, we had a huge spaghetti feed.

An event that was a highlight of the festival was a basketball tournament, which generated a lot of interest. The Alaska state troopers, under Swack's guidance, brought a team to town, as did the Homer Police Department. Port Graham put a team together and took part in the festival as did English Bay, now referred to as Nanwalek. Two teams were formed in Seldovia, and everyone had a great time. Wasilla joined us one year, when they brought a basketball team to town, which only added to a great time had by all. John Gruber headed up the basketball events. He made up all the brackets that outlined who played who and when they played, and he kept track of the winners of each game. He saw to it that the referees were on board, and the tournament was a huge success, mostly due to John Gruber's organizing skills and his hard work. John headed up the tournament every year for eight years, and the auditorium was always packed with fans and basketball teams. I had ordered trophies to award to the winners each year. After the tournament was over, we always had an Award's Banquet, and everyone said they were looking forward to the next year.

The festival always ended in the same way, with a talent show. I named the talent show "The Not So Ready for Prime-Time Talent Show," and I wrote a song with that title, and each year I opened with the song. I'm surprised everyone stayed for the rest of the show after having to sit through my guitar playing and singing.

The talent in this town was unbelievable. Every year, the show would last for three to four hours, with non-stop action. It did turn into somewhat of a "Roast," and I, for the most part, became the "Roastee." I should have taken the hint the first year, in 1981, when Gerry Willard came up on stage and awarded me a live little pig. The pig was wearing a tutu, and Pam Miller and Christine Kashevarof came on stage and presented me with a document they had prepared, which they said were adoption papers. They read the document to the crowd. They had named the pig "Rosebud," and I'll never forget what Gerry Willard said to the audience. He said, and I quote, "Who better to have a pig than your very own chief of police." Well, this brought the house down. The crowd loved the presentation. Me, not so much. Rosebud had visited the Linwood Bar prior to being presented to me. I heard Rick Harkness had given the oinker a large amount of beer prior to her being brought to the talent show. Of course, immediately upon my taking possession of the pig, she had to rid herself of a lot of the beer right on stage. I couldn't believe this was even happening, although I should have known Gerry would pull some kind of prank. What was I going to do with a pig? I had nowhere to house it, and I really hadn't planned a future that included a pig. After I recovered from the shock of the moment, I announced to the crowd that I would see to it the pig was raised and I would donate her to the upcoming July 4 activities for roasting. I received a mixed response to that statement.

Jack Thomas came to me after the talent show and told me he would house and raise Rosebud if I would supply the feed. I immediately agreed, and Rosebud grew to be around 500 pounds. Rick Harkness volunteered to take care of the preparation and the roasting of the animal. Gerry Willard, and others, assisted Rick, and they stayed up all night seeing to it that Rosebud was cooked perfectly.

Rosebud nearly escaped being butchered when some folks, not wanting to see her slaughtered, hid her from us when we went to pick her up. We were nearly in panic mode, when those hiding her finally gave up her location. To this day, I am still disappointed that, after spending all that money for pig food, I got busy with police work on the 4th of July and didn't even get a taste of, what was reportedly one delicious pig. I'm told Rosebud fed the masses, and everyone highly complimented the chef for a job well done.

Since we're talking about "Fuzz Ball," let me jump ahead and tell you a few more things that took place over the next few years during the "Not So Ready for Prime-Time Talent Show." The other events also took place with the basketball tournament, the old Seldovia movies, the kid games, the dinner, and other fun things like snowshoe baseball and snowshoe races but, everyone always looked forward to the talent show.

I felt the need to get even with Mr. Willard for his giving me Rose-bud. He adamantly denied being part of the initial plan and insisted he only was there to award the animal to me. Of course, I wasn't buying into that for a minute, and I was in revenge mode. I worked with a district attorney in 1981, by the name of Tom Wardell. Tom was one of the best attorneys I have ever worked with. He and his wife had a couple goats, and Tom told me he'd like to get rid of the nine-month-old neutered male. I told him I'd be tickled to death to take it off his hands. I told him what I was doing and guaranteed him the goat was going to a good home. Tom was definitely on board after hearing my plan.

The night of the talent show arrived, and I opened with the song I'd originally written for the show, and then I introduced a couple acts who took the stage and did their thing. I had an animal control officer working for me during that time, and I'd made arrangements for her to bring the goat up on stage when she heard the prearranged punchline. I had written another song, especially for Gerry. I do not recall all the lyrics but I do remember the last stanza. I told Janice Stone, my dog catcher, that when she heard the last stanza, she was to bring the goat up on stage. I played my guitar and sang the song to Gerry and then I sang the last stanza which was worded, "Instead of getting someone else's goat, here is one of your very own." Janice's timing was perfect. She brought the goat up on the stage right on cue, and Gerry, who was setting in a chair on stage looking bored, became very attentive when this nine-month-old neutered male goat turned, and walked right up to him like he was saying, "Hello Papa." The crowd absolutely lost it. They loved the fact that I'd gotten even with Gerry Willard by giving him a neutered male goat. A neutered nine-month-old goat is only good for two things, walking or eating. Unlike Rosebud, the town wouldn't ever let Gerry even consider putting that goat on a spit for barbequing.

A couple days after Gerry was awarded the goat, his wife told him she wanted a milk goat. Gerry reluctantly came to me and asked if the people I got the male goat from would possibly have a milk goat they would part with. I could see it was killing him to ask me this, and that only made it more enjoyable for me. I did check, and Mr. Wardell told me he had the mother of the Billy goat and, if I was serious, he would make arrangements to get it to Seldovia right away. I assured him I was serious, and within a couple weeks, Gerry and his wife, Alberta, were seen leading their two new pets around town on leashes. Throughout the summer, the Willard's were often seen leading the goats through town, and I have to say, I enjoyed it more and more each time I witnessed it. It was hilarious, and Gerry was such a good sport, but I often wondered if he ever got to where he liked goat milk but, then again, I was afraid to ask. I must admit I did worry about what he would come up with for the next Fuzzball talent show. I know he felt he had to retaliate, and as far as he was concerned, nothing was out of bounds.

The next year was another great Fuzzball Festival. Elaine Giles was at every basketball game and at every talent show, selling tickets at the door. She always had such a great time when she was a part of any function in Seldovia. She loved people, and everyone loved her. She was a vital part of the Fuzzball Festival and without the volunteers like her and John Gruber, the festival would never have gotten off the ground.

Gerry, as I was about to find out, had again been very busy, prior to the talent show, in his preparation to get even with me. He felt his retaliation for being given the goat would be great entertainment for the audience. This year he incorporated the Boy Scouts of our community in his antics. He had taken two poles, each being approximately ten inches long, and he attached a wire cage in the middle of the poles. This would enable the Boy Scouts to place the poles on their shoulders and, walking behind one another, carry the cage into the auditorium. Gerry had purchased a turkey and he placed it in the cage for his presentation. When he walked up on stage, he asked if he could make an announcement. I didn't know what was coming but I was extremely concerned about what he was up to. I reluctantly gave up the mic, and he immediately went into a spiel about drugs being too plentiful in our community. He said he felt the Seldovia Police Department didn't have the proper equipment to fight the problem, so he said he'd searched and searched and finally, he had located something he thought would help. He said he'd located a dope sniffing turkey. He told the crowd he wanted to award the bird to the police department to assist us in future drug investigations. It was then that the Boy Scouts, with poles on their shoulders, entered the auditorium, carrying the cage with the turkey inside. They walked to the front of the stage, between the stage and the audience, and set the cage down. The audience roared and applauded and applauded. Gerry, along with everyone else, was laughing and really enjoying his presentation. Gerry then turned to me and, without a word, and smiling ear to ear, handed me the mic. I just shook my head and I asked him if we were even yet. He said, "Probably not." I then explained to Gerry that the Fuzzball was all about making money for the police department for needed supplies, and a dope sniffing turkey wasn't in the budget. I told him I didn't want to feed another animal like I did Rosebud. I then addressed the audience and asked, "How much am I bid for a dope sniffing turkey?" Gerry's mouth dropped open and he had a look of total awe on his face. I was surprised when I started getting bids for the bird. If memory serves, I sold the turkey for $54.00. Everyone applauded, and I moved on with the talent show, bringing more acts on stage, one following the other, while the crowd continued to applaud each and every act.

Much to my dismay, Gerry wasn't done. It was getting toward the end of the talent show when Gerry again came up on the stage and asked if he could again address the crowd. Now I was scared. He had that look on his face that I had come to recognize when he was about to pull a prank. I, again, reluctantly gave up the mic, and Gerry again addressed the crowd. He told them the Seldovia Police Department was in dire need of dependable transportation. He went on and on, saying our police vehicles were old and we were having a lot of mechanical problems with them. He strung it out for what seemed like forever, making me more and more nervous, really fearing what was coming next. After what seemed like an eternity, Gerry had a friend lead a donkey out in front of the stage. The crowd went ballistic, and Gerry was having the time of his life. I whispered to him telling him, "You better be kidding on this one." He whispered back, telling me to go along with it, that I wasn't really getting the donkey. I relaxed a little after hearing that, but I still didn't trust him. He played it to the end. Gerry knew how to work the crowd. He talked about how the donkey would be very dependable transportation and he said it would relieve the city budget, in that we wouldn't have to buy gasoline in the future. He said, "Heck, we don't even have to worry about oil changes." He said he hoped he could find another one so both officer Bond and I would each have our own transportation. The crowd was roaring, and some comments were yelled out with statements like, "Is the donkey going to carry Andy or is he carrying the donkey?" I didn't really think it was all that funny, but the crowd sure loved it. Gerry had pulled it off again, but this time I didn't wind up with anything I had to feed. I was very pleased with how everything turned out.

After the show was over, Gerry told me he had borrowed the donkey from Willard's Farms, out of Homer, and the donkey was one of a matched pair. The owner told Gerry he enjoyed a good prank but, in no uncertain terms, the donkey better come back in the same shape as when he left the farm. The crowd literally loved Gerry's antics, and he was a huge part of what kept them coming back year after year. The talent show was a success again that year and for the next few years to come. Gerry and I made a pact between us that there would be no more animals presented to either of us, but we never really trusted the other to keep his word.

I really did miss a great opportunity when Gerry presented the donkey to me and I mentioned it to Gerry and Willie Flymm, the guy with the landing craft who'd delivered the donkey and was going to take it back. I asked Gerry, "What would you have done if I'd have said, what am I bid for this donkey?" Gerry said, "Oh my God!" Willie Flymm started laughing and said he personally would have bid Gerry up to $10,000.00 just because Gerry would have had to buy the animal back to see that it got back to Willard Farms. I told them I really missed my chance and it would have really been a crowd pleaser plus, I told them, look at the money I missed out on. Gerry said he really didn't see the humor in it but said he couldn't help being glad I was a slow thinker and didn't come up with the idea while I was still on stage.

The next morning, I received a call from Gerry telling me he needed help loading the donkey into the trailer that they were shipping it home in. I had mentioned to Gerry that my brother and I used to load reluctant horses into trailers and that there was a trick to it. I told Gerry I'd like to help him out but I was a slow thinker and would have to think about it for a while. He felt really bad about making that statement, he said. After we hung up, I responded and helped him load the animal. After we had the donkey loaded and tied to the front of the trailer, the animal started pawing at the trailer's plywood floor. I noticed this and told Gerry that I hoped he didn't paw a hole in the floor of the trailer. Gerry got a look of fear in his eyes and just shook his head. The trailer with the donkey aboard was loaded onto the landing craft, and Willie got underway to Homer. Gerry said a lineman friend, whom he named, was going to deliver the donkey back to Willard Farms. I bid Gerry farewell and I went home.

As I was relaxing at home, following all the festivities, I suddenly had an idea. It was as if a light bulb had gone off. I got on the phone and called the lineman Gerry said was delivering the donkey to Willard Farms. I knew the man and I asked him if he'd like to pull a prank on Gerry Willard. He said, "You bet," and he asked me what I had in mind. I told him about the donkey pawing at the floor of the trailer and I said he should call Gerry, after he delivered the animal to Willard Farms, and tell him the donkey pawed a hole in the floor of the trailer and he'd gotten his leg down in the hole and they had dragged his leg off when transporting him to Willard Farms. The lineman said he loved the idea and said he'd make it very convincing. I told him not to tell Gerry any different and I'd let him sweat for a while before I let him off the hook.

The plan was in place, and now all I had to do was wait for a phone call from Gerry. It was approximately another two hours before Gerry called me. He told me I'd never believe what happened. He said the donkey had pawed a hole in the floor of the trailer and had gotten his leg dragged off on the road when he fell into it. Gerry said he really didn't know what to do, because that donkey was one of a matching pair and he was dearly loved by his owner. Playing it to the hilt I said,

"You got to be kidding me, aren't you?" He told me that the lineman had called him and he wasn't kidding. I told him I didn't know what he should do but it sounded to me like he was going to have to come up with some mega-bucks to cover this one. I could tell by his voice that he was really suffering so, after a little while, I let him off the hook. I just said, "Gotcha." He was quiet for a short time and then told me that this was a really dirty trick to play on a friend. I told him, if given the chance, he would have done the same thing to me but he would have kept me hanging a lot longer than I did him. The stress had left his voice and I could tell he was no longer about to have a coronary. I laughed and told him, "Mess with me, buddy, just mess with me." He told me he'd talk to me later, and we terminated the call. I do have to say I felt a little bad for him for half a second but it faded really quickly.

It was a couple years later that I called the Monkey Warf in Anchorage and tried to buy a monkey that I could present to Gerry during the talent show. I planned to write him another song, about monkeying around with people, but the Monkey Warf said they would not sell just one monkey but they would sell me all of them. I told them I wasn't interested in buying a bunch of monkeys. I felt I should tell Gerry about my efforts and when I did, he said that was the same thing they told him when he called, trying to buy me a monkey. I told him, "Wow, great minds do think alike, I guess." I've often wondered what would have happened if they'd had sold each of us a monkey. I don't think it would have ended well at all.

The Fuzzball Festivals, over the years, did generate a lot of money, and Elaine Giles had a Fuzzball account opened for those funds. Since the money was generated by the police department, and monies collected were for police use, I had total control over what it was spent on. I was able to get a professional camera outfit, including numerous lenses, and all the bells and whistles. I bought investigative kits, a fuming tank, and a lot more equipment to aid us in upcoming investigations. The funds were to be used for items that would benefit the citizens of Seldovia. Sadly, a local young man drowned when he was washed overboard on the west side of Cook Inlet in the Kamashak area while king crab fishing. The AST conducted an extensive search but, after a time, they suspended the search, having not located the body. The family was still holding out hope that their family member's remains could be found and brought home. Due to the importance of this to the family, I was hopeful that I could possibly assist them in getting closure, so I called Larry Thompson, owner/operator of Homer Air Service in Homer, and asked if we could fly the Kamashak area to search for the young man. Larry, being a personal friend of the family as well, and being aware of the incident, readily agreed. I had a couple friends join us, and the next day we flew in one of Larry's Aztec twin-engine aircrafts. We spent over two and a half hours searching, but to no avail. I felt the cost of the flight should be paid through Fuzzball funds as the money was for the benefit of a local family. Larry Thompson, feeling as I did, split the cost with me. We were both saddened that we couldn't bring the young man home.

The Fuzzball funds again came in handy in the fall of the year, when the Rocky River Road washed out, making it impassable for any vehicular traffic. I had a concerned party contact me and ask me if I knew if any motorhomes, who visited Rocky River, had gotten out before the road washed out. I had no way of knowing, not knowing who all were alleged to have been in that area. I called trooper Bayes of the Alaska State Troopers and shared the man's concerns with him. The trooper asked if anyone knew if people were trapped or were they just questioning the fact that someone may be trapped. I told him they were only posing a question, wondering if anyone was trapped. The trooper told me the case didn't meet the criteria needed to warrant spending the money on a search. He said it was not a search and rescue and the state wouldn't fly the area just to satisfy someone's curiosity. I understood the State's reasoning, but I felt it was important enough to warrant my spending Fuzzball funds to ensure no one was trapped behind the washout. I again called Larry Thompson, and this time we flew the area in a Cessna 206. We didn't find any evidence of anyone being caught behind the washout, which was a relief, knowing every-one had gotten out before the storm. I didn't feel bad about spending the Fuzzball funds in this effort. I strongly felt this was the type of expenditure the Fuzzball funds were all about.

I'm very sad to report that both Gerry Willard and Elaine Giles have passed away, and everyone who knew them misses them greatly. They were both unique people, each with very caring and loving hearts. They always treated people with respect and admiration and, in turn, they were treated with respect and admiration. Both were very active in the politics of the city of Seldovia. Elaine was the city clerk/treasurer for many years. Gerry held positions of mayor, councilman, and on three occasions, took the interim city manager's seat while the council was searching for a new candidate. Both were prime examples of why I love Seldovia so much. I think of them often as I'm sure, do most of the older Seldovians. Gerry and Elaine will always be remembered as being a huge part of the heart of our city. Rest in peace, my friends.

Burglaries of Seldovia Businesses

The Fuzzball was over, and day to day operations continued in the police department. Both Officer Bond and I kept very busy with all that was going on.

On February 24, 1981, a report of a burglary at Pacific Pearl Seafoods was received; apparently $912.48 was reportedly taken. On March 18, 1981, burglary of John's Sport Shop was received; entry was made through the back door of the business. A total of $1327.91 was reportedly taken along with some tools, worth approximately $65.00. On April 18, 1981, the Knight Spot Bar was burglarized, and $382.00 was reportedly missing. On the same date, three more burglaries in businesses were reported. The Standard Oil Company reported $40.00 in cash and $144.94 in checks taken. The Linwood Bar was forcibly entered, and $80.00 in cash and coin, was taken, and the SBE School was also forcibly entered with $690.00 in cash reportedly missing. It was evident to the investigating officers that most probably the same person, or persons, were responsible for most, if not all, the burglaries. The two burglaries in February and March occurred while I was in town, but I was gone from April 15 to May 30, when the other burglaries took place. Upon my return, I continued to investigate the unsolved burglaries.

Officer Bond left the department at the beginning of April, and we brought in Officer O'Dean Hall to cover the department in my absence. It appeared the burglar(s) took advantage of the fact that a new officer was in town. Three of the five burglaries occurred on Officer Hall's watch. Officer Hall was a certified police officer and he knew his job. Being in a small town, and not knowing anyone, were definitely obstacles, but that didn't stop Officer Hall. He developed a few suspects and his persistence dissuaded any further burglaries. However, the fingerprints he had lifted at the scene of two of the three burglaries weren't of any evidentiary value. Most often, a burglar will wear gloves, and the fingerprints Officer Hall lifted could have been most anyone's. A burglary can be one of the most difficult crimes to solve, but when a couple are solved in a small community, it usually winds up being the same party or parties doing most, if not all, of the break-ins. The five burglary cases were kept open, and the investigations continued.

Officer Hall did make numerous arrests for driving while intoxicated, assault and disorderly conduct and in the six weeks he was in town, he showed the community what it was like to have a police officer who went by the book, knew what he was doing, and was aggressive in his enforcement. He was one who wouldn't back down if accosted and he would follow up on open cases. He developed a lot of enemies in his six weeks of service but he did a great job and he did keep the peace in Seldovia while I was gone. I might add that all the arrests Officer Hall made were found guilty when they went before the court. My thanks to the officer for filling in for me.

MUNICIPAL ACADEMY #19

Captain Swackhammer, Swack, contacted me in January of 1981, prior to the Fuzzball Festival, and asked if I'd be interested in getting some training in law enforcement. I, of course, told him I really would appreciate learning how to do the job the right way. I'm sure he had heard about the lawsuit I'd been named in, but he never once mentioned it. He said he'd get back to me but he'd see what he could do about getting me into the next Municipal Police Academy (MPA), which was coming up in April of this year. I told him I'd need to clear it with my boss, in that the expense could very well be more than the city wanted to spend. Swack told me he'd see that all expenses were paid by the DPS if the city would continue to pick up my wages. He said DPS would pay all costs, including the airfare to and from Sitka, and all expenditures associated with my training at the Academy. I told him I'd talk to the city manager and I would get back to him, and I told him how much I appreciated his assistance in getting me some training. I checked it out with the city manager, and he said he didn't see a problem with the city paying my wages while I was being trained but, again, he would have to take it before the city council for approval. At the next council meeting, the city manager did inform the council of the offer by Captain Swackhammer, and they unanimously agreed to continue paying my wages while I was in Sitka at the Alaska State Troopers Academy.

I contacted Swack and told him the good news, and he said he'd get to work on setting it up. He told me I'd be receiving some forms I needed to fill out for enrollment purposes. Swack again came through for the city of Seldovia, saving them a bundle of money in training costs and, hopefully, ensuring them that they would not be dealing with any more lawsuits due to the fact their chief of police didn't know what he was doing. With the DPS contract in effect, my lack of training was most probably of great concern to AST as well.

In our small town, news moves quickly, and everyone I came in contact with mentioned the fact I was going to finally get some police training. They all were just kidding me, but I felt the training was way overdue. Prior to going to Sitka, I was contacted by Norman Kashevarof, another Seldovian, who was now into commercial fishing, but he had served in the chief's position for a couple years and had gone through the MPA in Sitka. What he told me was some of the best advice I ever received in reference to the citizens of Seldovia. He said I should remember I would be changed in Sitka due to the training but, he said, "The people in Seldovia will not change and they will be the same when you get back. Remember that when it comes to enforcement here at home." I've thought of this a lot over the years, and he was right. I did have a different outlook when I came home but, due to his advice, I reined in that "Go Get Em" attitude and just tried to do my job. I still believe I was hired to protect and serve the people, not to harass or bully anyone. I hope the majority of the public feel that I have conducted myself professionally and fairly and they didn't feel bullied or mistreated under my watch.

On April 15, I found myself in Sitka enlisted in MPA 19 at the Alaska State Trooper Police Academy. The Academy was structured much like a military boot camp. We were up nearly every morning doing calisthenics and running. We would have physical training (PT) for an hour and then hit the showers before going to breakfast. After breakfast, we went to the classroom where, over the next six weeks, we would be schooled in all aspects of law enforcement. I enjoyed the time spent in the classroom because it was so informative. The instructors were all professionals and made it very clear that no question was out of bounds, and they encouraged us to speak up if we didn't understand something. Every instructor I found to be very well schooled in the subject matter they were teaching. One of the most enjoyable classes for me was when we went to the shooting range. We would shoot two to three times weekly, and our instructor, Alaska State Trooper Don Savage, taught us the proper way to shoot a handgun. He was very good at what he did; his manner of teaching was straightforward and he would take the time with anyone struggling. I actually went from shooting in the mid-50s to shooting in the upper-90s by the end of my time at the academy.

With a couple days to go before my time was over; we had a shooting competition. I was shooting my Smith & Wesson 357 revolver and I was using speed loaders to reload. This made a lot of difference in the range when we were going against the clock. At these timed shoots, we were given a time limit in which to finish at each station. There was a total of seven stations in all, with each being closer to the target than the last. At each station we were to shoot six rounds, reload, and shoot six more rounds, making a total of twelve shots at each location. I was feeling really good with my shooting thus far as we advanced to the 7½ yard line. At this distance, it was very easy to put all 12 rounds in the bullseye, but we had considerably less time to shoot all twelve rounds than at the other stations. This was always a concern for the shooters, adding additional stress to the competition. I was feeling really good about how it was going but I was nervous at the 7½ yard line, knowing I needed to finish before time ran out. When the bell sounded, I shot six shots, each hitting the center of the target, then I reached for my speed loader. Somehow, when I took the speed loader out of its carrier, I dumped all six rounds, and I had to pick them up off the ground and reload them by hand. I loaded the revolver as quickly as I could and was able to get off two shots before the bell sounded, ending all shooting. I still wound up with a score of 94 but another officer beat me out with a score of 98. I know, had I not dumped the six rounds on the ground, I would not have run out of time, and I would have scored higher than the officer scoring the 98. But for the screwup, I would have won the competition. Trooper

Savage talked to me after the competition and he agreed that I would most probably have won had I not dumped the speed loader. He said the course was built in such a way as to put the officer under stress when he was shooting. Oh well, second place isn't bad, and I did learn how to shoot, and that was the most important thing.

After I graduated from the academy, I was really glad to get back home. I met some great men and women who have remained friends throughout my police career. I have stayed in touch with many of them over the years. Trooper Don Savage has visited me in Seldovia on a couple occasions, and we had lunch and reminisced about old times. I also returned home 26 pounds lighter than when I'd left, due to all the exercise I was getting. It didn't seem like any time at all before I was able to put back those 26 pounds I'd lost in Sitka. I was amazed at how it followed me home.

The first day I was back home, I was driving down the street in my patrol vehicle, with my window rolled down, when a man, an extremely intoxicated fisherman, and a friend of mine, flagged me down. After I stopped the vehicle, he grabbed me with a hand on each side of my cheeks, and he kissed me right on the lips. He caught me totally off guard. He said he was so happy I was home and I could never leave again. He had been a subject of Officer Hall's enforcement and he didn't have too many good things to say about him. Needless to say, I nearly lost my lunch but I did realize how much he thought of me. It was good to be home, but I would be very alert from now on, and I'd be watching for another attack.

OFFICER JERRY L. LEWIS JOINS THE FORCE

In June 1981, after I'd returned from police training at Alaska State Trooper Academy, I approached the city manager and the city council, making them aware of the need for another patrol officer, due to the caseload the Seldovia PD was carrying. I was being called on day and night by people needing assistance. Thankfully, the council recognized the problem and gave a green light for the funding of a patrol officer position. Jerry Lee Lewis, no, not the piano player, came to Seldovia to apply for the job. Jerry was the chief of police in Whitter, Alaska at the time and he told me he was ready for a change. He said the politics in Whitter had become overwhelming and he was totally burned out from fighting City Hall. He shared with me that he just wanted to find a department where he could do police work and let someone else handle all the politics. Jerry had been in law enforcement for most of his adult life and, after he was hired, I found out how much he really knew about law enforcement.

When a man goes through an academy, he learns basic law. When he hits the streets, he learns how to apply the law. Officer Lewis became my Field Training Officer (FTO), so to speak, and I drew from his knowledge as I learned how to apply some of the rules on the street. I found his knowledge invaluable and will always hold Officer Lewis in the highest esteem for sharing what he knew with me. Jerry had a unique way of approaching almost all police situations. He'd been involved in so many different situations during his law enforcement career, that he knew how to bring most of them to completion in a quarter of the time it would take me. He and I kept very busy during the next seven years while he was an officer in the Seldovia PD, and I owe him more than I can ever thank him for.

If Officer Lewis was looking for a slower pace than he'd had in Whitter, he soon realized we had our fair share of cases, as well. The caseload is somewhat surprising for most people, with the population being as low as it was. In 1981 alone, we had eight DWI's, three cases of criminal mischief, two charged with furnishing liquor to minors, seven minors were charged with minors possessing alcohol, ten burglaries were investigated, there were three cases involving marijuana, three disorderly conduct investigations, four theft reports, two people charged with resisting arrest, two reports of shooting in the city limits, and two harassment investigations. We investigated four vehicle accidents and one report of a hit & run. These crimes and infractions didn't include the hours and hours of traffic patrol and assistance calls from the public. The bar checks and the mounds of paperwork it takes to record the daily activities of a police department take an overwhelming amount of time. Some of the investigations took literally days to complete as did the following marijuana case we investigated.

FURNISHING MARIJUANA TO MINORS

On December 10, 1981, at approximately 2130 hours, while making rounds in the area of the airport, I drove up near the small dam located on Fish Creek. I observed a vehicle parked in a pullout and thought it to be somewhat suspicious. I exited my police vehicle and went over to the car, where I found four juveniles inside. The driver's door was damaged and could not be opened and the window couldn't be rolled down. The vehicle had a wing window, and the driver opened it. As soon as he opened the wing window, I was hit in the face with a very strong odor of marijuana. I walked to the passenger side of the vehicle and opened the front door, ordering the two occupants to exit from the front seat. I told the other two juveniles in the back seat to stay put. As the two exited, I asked who had the marijuana, and the driver handed me a piece of paper that held marijuana. He had twisted the top, sealing the marijuana inside. The two rear-seat passengers exited, and all were searched. The only marijuana that was found was that held by the driver. I asked if any more drugs were in the vehicle, and the driver told me that what I had was all the marijuana they had. I asked if the driver would mind if I searched the vehicle, and he told me to go ahead. I checked the vehicle and didn't find any more marijuana or other illegal drugs. I then loaded three of the four juveniles into my vehicle and told the driver of the other vehicle to drive to the police department. I told all of them they were under arrest for possession of a controlled substance, and I warned the young man driving the vehicle that he would be charged with escape if he did not show up at the police department at the same time the rest of us did.

After reaching the PD, I got all of the young men's personal information for the paperwork, after which I called each one of their parents. I requested the parents to come to the PD where their child could be released into their custody. The parents arrived at the PD within half an hour, and each were filled in on what had taken place. I explained they would have to accompany their child when they met with the Juvenile Intake Officer, Eric Weatherby. I told them he would be taking over their cases. Each juvenile was then released into their parents' custody. All of the parents were angry and were telling their child what they could expect when they got them home.

In the State of Alaska, the Juvenile Intake System handles all criminal cases wherein a minor, under the age of eighteen is involved. The investigating agency investigates the crimes and makes arrests, or files charges in the case, but the juvenile intake officer has the final say. It is a lot like the district attorney's office for adults. Eric Weatherby and Karen Rogers were the intake officers for the Kenai Peninsula. After a case is turned over to the juvenile intake officers, the PD has little control at that point, and rarely do we receive any adjudication reports.

After all the juveniles had been released into the custody of their parents, I unwrapped the paper the marijuana was wrapped in so I could weigh it. The marijuana weighed ¼ ounce and I bagged it in a plastic sandwich bag. I was also going to log the paper which held the marijuana into evidence when I noticed it was a letter written to a local juvenile who was stateside for the winter. I started reading the letter; it described where the marijuana had come from and the many times the author of the letter, and other juveniles, had been given marijuana by the man growing it. The writer named a 64-year-old man, stating he was distributing the drugs to the kids. I was well acquainted with the suspect, in that we had been watching him for over a year. We had gained intelligence that he was hanging with juveniles and never in the presence of adults, which is a definite red flag. The suspect had lived on a boat during the winter of 80/81 and, in the summer of 1981, he purchased a small 19'–20' pull-type trailer, which he moved out of town and was now living in. The letter went on to say the suspect had built a visquine structure around his trailer and had grown a bunch of marijuana. It was all dried now, and he was just giving it to any kid who wanted some, the letter read.

I immediately called Cpl. Dennis Oakland of the Homer Police Department and told him what I had run across. Cpl. Oakland and I were both members of the South-Central Area Narcotics Team (SCAN), and this was the type case the team was interested in. Cpl. Oakland asked that I fax over the information regarding the case and he said he'd apply for a search warrant to search the suspect's residence and/ or any other structures on his property, including his personal vehicle. The corporal told me not to do anything to alert the man; we would just show up and serve the search warrant.

Both Cpl. Oakland and I were rookies when it came to being part of the SCAN unit, but we had both been in law enforcement long enough to know what we had to do to make a case that would interest the district attorney.

A day had passed when Cpl. Oakland called me and told me he had the search warrant in hand and would be in Seldovia at 1015 hours that morning. He asked if Officer Lewis would be available to assist in the search, and I told him that he wouldn't miss this for the world.

Sgt. Gene Kallus of the Alaska State Troopers headed up the SCAN Team out of the Soldotna Post for AST. After I returned from the Sitka Troopers Academy, he had traveled to Seldovia to introduce himself and invite me to join the SCAN Team. I, of course, jumped at the chance to be part of the team. I immediately liked Sgt. Kallus and found him to be upbeat, jovial, and very well-schooled in drug interdiction and eradication. Sgt. Kallus would be very happy to hear about this case, provided it turned out as we hoped it would.

Cpl. Oakland arrived in Seldovia, and we picked him up at the airport. Officer Lewis drove his police vehicle out to the suspect's residence, and I transported Cpl. Oakland in mine. Upon reaching the residence, we observed a large visquine covered structure that was attached to the end and the side of his trailer. We had to walk inside the structure to get to the trailer door. Upon knocking, our suspect opened the door. He seemed a little taken back on seeing three police officers at his door. I greeted him and told him we had a search warrant to search his home, outbuildings, and his vehicle for marijuana and/or other drugs. The suspect said he only had marijuana and no other drugs. He invited us in, and I told him to have a seat while we searched his home. I supplied him with a copy of the warrant. He sat down and, on a number of different occasions, he told one of us where more marijuana was located. He was very helpful throughout the search. The marijuana inside the trailer had been processed and had been put in clear plastic sandwich bags. Everywhere we looked, we observed another bag, or numerous bags, of marijuana.

After we had collected all the marijuana inside the trailer, I directed the suspect to come out into the visquine structure with us. I had him take a seat on a bench by the trailer's door. In the visquine structure, there were plants hanging upside down to dry and other plants still in their pots, still growing. Cpl. Oakland and I started pulling the marijuana plants while Officer Lewis collected the ones hanging upside down, drying. All the marijuana collected in the search was put in plastic garbage bags. At one point, when Cpl. Oakland and I were pulling the plants, the suspect yelled for us to quit pulling his tomato plants. We were so caught up in the pulling of the marijuana plants, we never recognized some of the plants to be tomato plants that we were pulling. It was a little embarrassing, to say the least. Being raised on a farm, I think I was more embarrassed than was Cpl. Oakland. We apologized and then refrained from pulling any more tomato plants. I think it'll be a long time, if ever, before we live that one down.

The collected marijuana was loaded into the police vehicle, and we arrested the suspect and transported him, and the drugs, to the Seldovia Police Department. Cpl. Oakland called the airlines and made arrangements for a flight back to Homer. Officer Lewis provided transportation to the airport for the Corporal and the suspect, and Cpl. Oakland took the suspect to the Homer Jail.

I logged all the evidence in and then packaged it and sent it to the AST Laboratory in Anchorage. When the laboratory got back to me,

I found we had collected 1,260 grams, or 2.778 pounds, of marijuana, and it all tested positive for the presence of THC.

The suspect pled guilty when he went before the court and he was sentenced to five years in jail with three years suspended. When he was released, he would be on probation for five years and would have to keep in monthly contact with his probation officer. He was to have no contact with juveniles under the age of eighteen, and he was ordered to undergo drug treatment. I understand the man passed away shortly after getting out of jail, thus ensuring he would not return to his old ways.

Eric Weatherby, juvenile intake officer, was forwarded the case and he came to Seldovia and met with the juveniles and their parents. What came of it, I don't know. We usually weren't notified what the sentence or any court actions taken in juvenile cases were. (Case Closed by Arrest)

1982: A Busy Year in the Seldovia Police Department

I n 1982, the Seldovia Police Department was kept very busy with myriad crimes and infractions. Investigations were conducted for a felony assault, three misdemeanor assaults, two cases of furnishing liquor to minors, with eight minors being charged with minor in possession of alcohol. There were eight driving while intoxicated cases, three disorderly conduct cases, and three criminal mischief cases, while three thefts were reported. Four motor vehicle accidents were investigated while one aircraft accident occurred. Two negligent driving investigations were conducted, and one hit & run was reported. One obscene conduct was charged. Three burglaries occurred, and one man was arrested on a bench warrant.

The city dock was damaged by the state ferry, Tustumena, upon landing and I was present at the time. Part of my responsibilities included tying up the state ferry when it arrived. It was approximately 0850 hours on May 27, 1982, when the ferry was approaching the Seldovia dock. The wind was out of the southeast at approximately 15 mph. Due to the wind, the Tustumena was being blown toward the dock at a greater speed than is usual when docking. Rollins Construction Co. had been working on the city dock, driving new pilings. There was a new piling in place, ready to be driven, standing up on the southeast end of the dock. Other new pilings had already been driven in that location.

When the Tustumena hit the southeast end of the dock, a large cracking sound was heard and I felt the dock sway due to the impact. After hitting the southeast corner of the dock, momentum carried the Tustumena in a forward direction. Another piling, which had been set in place to be driven, was hit with the davit, which supports the gangway. The davit sustained damage at that point, as did the piling.

After the boat was secured to the dock, the captain came ashore and asked what all was damaged. The city manager had arrived on the dock by this time, and the Rollins Construction crew was present and witnessed the landing as well. A header block was observed to be busted, and the captain checked it and stated it had sawdust and small gravel in the busted area, so he said it was damaged prior to his docking and he wasn't taking responsibility for that damage. Carl Hille, the city manager, asked Richard Rollins, the crew foreman, if he had noticed the damage to the header block prior to the Tustumena docking. Mr. Rollins told the manager that the crew had been working in that area and he felt, if the header block was previously busted, they would have noticed it.

On May 31, 1982, at approximately 1400 hours, Carl Hille, Helen Hille, Richard Rollins, and I surveyed the damage to the dock at low tide out of a skiff. Considerable damage was found to the pilings in the southeast corner of the dock. A new piling, which had just been driven, was found to be busted in half and another new piling, just to the northeast of the damaged one, appeared to be broken below the waterline. That piling had been slid eight to ten feet. The break was not visible, due to the water obscuring it, but it was apparent it had been damaged by the impact of the ferry. Helen Hille took photographs of the damaged area, and I was directed, by the city manager, to do a police report on what I had witnessed and all the damage I had observed. Photographs of the damage to the header block and the damage sustained to the pilings above the dock had been taken shortly after the mishap.

As directed, I filled out a police report and turned it into the city office. I was never called on to testify at any hearing, and the matter was never discussed between the city manager and me again. Because no further discussion occurred, I think it's safe to assume the city and the state came to an equitable agreement. To date, I've never heard anything more about that incident. (Case Closed by Report)

CRIMINAL MISCHIEF AND A MENTAL COMMITMENT

It was January 1, 1982, at approximately 1630 hours, when I received a call from the bartender at the Seldovia Lodge. She said the police were needed at the bar right away. She said an unruly customer, who came in intoxicated, had ordered a drink, and she had refused to serve him. He got angry and kicked the glass out of the jukebox, damaging the plastic background. She said he was disruptive and was picking on all the customers, trying to start a fight. I told the bartender I would be there shortly.

I geared up and responded to the Lodge after calling a friend, Gerry Willard, and asking if he would assist me. Officer Lewis was out of town at the time. I knew the suspect and had dealt with him on numerous occasions. When he was sober, he was jovial and was always joking around, but when he was intoxicated, he could be a holy terror. When intoxicated, he was very aggressive and had to be dealt with very firmly. He abused both alcohol and drugs, and he had attempted suicide on a couple occasions by overdosing on pills.

In my police career, I rarely had to go hands-on with anyone, but this suspect was different. You couldn't reason with him at all when he was intoxicated. I learned early in my career that the most important weapon in an officer's arsenal is the area below his nose and above his chin. But, in this case, I was pretty sure this response would not end without an altercation taking place because, when he was intoxicated, no one could reason with him.

I arrived at the Seldovia Lodge at approximately 1645 hours. I observed the broken glass in the jukebox and the damaged plastic background. The suspect was at the bar, sitting beside a patron and was cursing him. I went to the end of the bar and talked with the bartender. I asked how long he'd been in the bar, and she said he'd come in and immediately ordered the drink and, when turned down, he'd kicked the glass out of the jukebox. This happened right before she called me, she stated. I asked if she was willing to sign a "Citizen's Arrest Form," since it was a misdemeanor that hadn't happened in my presence. She said she would but told me I needed to get him out of the bar. I told her I'd get her a form and bring it to her after I had the suspect taken care of. I was hoping he would go quietly but I really doubted that would be the case. Gerry Willard arrived at the bar, and I was glad to see him, knowing I would most probably have problems with the suspect.

I walked up to the suspect and told him he needed to come with me, that he was intoxicated, and he couldn't be in a bar drunk. He told me to go to hell and just sat on his stool. I told him we could do this easy or we could do it the hard way, and I preferred the easy way. Gerry was standing on the other side of the suspect. I told the suspect he knew me well enough to know I wasn't kidding. He swung round on his stool and tried to push me away. When he reached out, I grabbed his arm, pulling him off the stool and I took him to the floor. I quickly put him face down and, with him fighting me, I was able to get a handcuff on his right wrist; then, with Gerry's assistance, we had to wrestle his other arm out from under him. We were finally able to get the other wrist cuffed up, and I just sat there, on him, catching my breath. As soon as the second cuff was on, the suspect quit fighting. After I caught my breath, we helped the suspect up, with him cursing us out. We headed out of the bar to the police vehicle. When we reached the vehicle, the suspect started pulling away and this time, he was trying to kick me. With Gerry's assistance, we were able to get the suspect loaded into the front passenger seat of the patrol vehicle.

I put a seat belt around him, with him still kicking and trying to kick the at radio and shotgun rack. I asked Mr. Willard if he would be able to assist me in transporting the suspect. I told him Officer Lewis was out of town so I had to call on him. He said he knew how the suspect could be and he would help me as long as I needed him to.

After we had the suspect loaded, I called my wife on the VHF radio and asked that she call the doctor and have him meet us at the clinic. My line of thought was that the doctor may be able to give the suspect something that would calm him down, and we could deal with the problem without getting into a wrestling match or even worse.

As we were getting underway to the clinic, the suspect again started kicking at the radio and the shotgun rack. I had to stop the vehicle and subdue him physically, holding his legs down to make him stop kicking. He calmed down after a time, and we started out again en route to the clinic. Gerry was sitting behind the suspect in the back seat, and when the suspect would start kicking, there was nothing Mr. Willard could do to stop him. When we again started for the clinic, the suspect again started kicking; this time he kicked at the windshield. I immediately stopped the vehicle and again physically subdued him. I asked Mr. Willard to get a short line I kept in the back of the patrol vehicle, and I tied it around the suspect's legs, hobbling him. I left the short end of the line hanging outside but under the door, so when the door was closed, it would act as an anchor for the line. The suspect was restrained to the point he couldn't do anything now. He was handcuffed behind his back, he was in a seatbelt, and his legs were hobbled. We were then able to drive to the clinic without any further problems.

We reached the clinic prior to the doctor arriving. The suspect said his legs hurt and he wanted to stand up outside while we waited on the doctor. I felt there would be less problems if I gave in to the suspect in this regard, so I took the hobbles off and got him out of the vehicle. He immediately tried to pull away from me and started trying to kick me again. I took him to the ground and held him down until the doctor arrived. The suspect complained that I had hurt his arm and leg when I took him down so, after the doctor arrived, I explained to him what had transpired and I asked that he check the suspect for injuries to his arms and legs. The suspect was examined by the doctor and he did find a scrape or two had been sustained in the scuffle, but the doctor didn't think there were any serious injuries.

The doctor and I discussed the mental state of the suspect and we both agreed he should have a psychiatric evaluation. I asked the doctor if he would write a short note to that effect and sign and date it. I told him I would then fill out an "Officer's Mental Commitment Form," and we could possibly get the suspect held on a 72-hour mental commitment hold where he would be evaluated.

Another problem that had to be dealt with was, due to inclement weather, no airplanes were flying. It was now 1810 hours and was already dark. The snow was coming down and there was no way an airplane was going to fly. In planning what to do next, I called the suspect's brother-in-law, who I felt could physically restrain the suspect if it came to that, and I asked if he would mind spending the night with the suspect as a guard. We would let them stay at the suspect's apartment, at the Seldovia Lodge, if he would guard him. The suspect's brother-in-law agreed and said he'd meet us at the Lodge.

Gerry and I transported the suspect back to the Seldovia Lodge, where we were met by the suspect's brother-in-law. I gave the brother-in-law a handheld VHF radio and told him to call me if the suspect got out of hand or caused him any trouble. I told him I'd check in on him later in the evening.

With no jail facility, one had to be creative in some instances. This was one of those times. I felt we had to have someone we could depend on, as well as someone who could physically restrain the suspect if he got out of control, and the brother-in-law fit that criteria.

It was just after 2100 hours when the brother-in-law called me on the handheld radio and said I should come to the suspect's room. He reported that the suspect was becoming violent, and he had to restrain him. I geared up and responded to the suspect's room at the Seldovia Lodge. When I entered the room, I observed the brother-in-law had placed the suspect back in the handcuffs, which I'd left with him, and he was holding him down on the floor. He told me the suspect told him he was going to get a drink and he'd gone to the cupboard and opened it in an attempt to get a bottle of vodka. The brother-in-law had stopped him and had to wrestle with him to keep him from getting the vodka and he'd been able, after a tussle, to get him back into handcuffs. He said he decided he'd to just hold him down on the floor until I arrived.

We got the suspect up onto his feet and we loaded him into the patrol vehicle again. This time, I hobbled him in the same fashion I had earlier, prior to taking him to the police department. I decided I was through playing his game. After we arrived at the PD, which was located in the city hall complex, I had the brother-in-law sit with the suspect in my office while I went out into the shop area. I located a log chain. The firetruck and ambulance, belonging to the city, were both stored in the warehouse across from one another, leaving a space of approximately 20 feet between them. Both vehicles were chained up due to the winter conditions. I fastened one end of the log chain to the chain on the rear tire of the ambulance and I fastened the other end of the log chain to the rear chain on the firetruck. I had an army cot stored at the warehouse and I placed it in the middle over the top of the log chain. After I had it rigged, I called for the brother-in-law to bring the suspect out to the warehouse. I took one side of the hand-cuffs off the suspect's wrist and cuffed him to the chain, close to the cot so he could lie down and still have room to move around a little. The first thing the suspect did was to kick the cot away from him. I thought, "Well, that didn't work." I was somewhat irritated with this whole matter and then, I had an idea. I put the cot back in place, over the top of the chain, and then made the suspect set down on the cot. After he sat down, I took the second set of handcuffs and handcuffed his other arm to the chain on the other side of the cot. He now could not rise and he couldn't kick the cot away. This is how he spent the night, handcuffed to the chain. It sounds somewhat inhumane, but the situation was such that it required extreme measures be taken to secure the suspect and keep him, and everyone else, safe from harm. The suspect did injure both wrists during the night, when he kept pulling on the chain with one arm and then the other. I asked his brother-in-law what he thought about the set up, and he said he shouldn't have any further problems now. He did ask if he could be relieved around 0400 hours, so he could get some rest, and I told him I'd see if could find someone to relieve him.

After I left the brother-in-law and the suspect, I went back to the Seldovia Lodge and took a "Citizen's Arrest Form" to them to be signed. The owner of the bar was there at that time, and he signed the form and stated he wanted his jukebox fixed. I told him the court would have to address that. I then left and went to my residence.

After I arrived home, I called a close friend, John Gruber, and asked if he would be available to watch the suspect from 0400 hours until after daylight, and he said he would. John relieved the brother-in-law at 0400 hours, and we had no further problems with the suspect.

I'd known John Gruber since 1964, when I first arrived in Seldovia, and we were good friends. Throughout the years, when I found myself without a patrol officer, I would call on John, and he would accompany me on any calls wherein I felt backup could be needed. He was always calm and he was always vigilant, ready to take whatever steps necessary to assist me in any given situation. We had a few memorable incidents I'm sure he could tell you all about.

The next morning, I called Trooper Bruce Bayes of the Alaska State Troopers, and I told him what had occurred, and the steps I had taken. He told me to transport the prisoner to Homer and he'd meet me and lock him up in the Homer Jail. He told me to bring the note from the doctor, and we'd go before the court with the "Officer's Committal Form" and see if we'd get a mental commitment hold. If the hold was ordered, the troopers would transport the suspect to the Alaska Psychiatric Institute (API) in Anchorage.

When I relieved John Gruber the following morning, the suspect had sobered up and was a lot more congenial than he had been the night before. I told the suspect what the plan was, and he told me he wouldn't cause any more trouble. The airplane was called, and I transported the suspect without incident. Trooper Bayes met the airplane, and we responded to the Homer Jail where the suspect was booked in. We then went to the Homer Court. I went before the judge and gave her the note from the doctor and the "Officer's Mental Commitment

Form," and I told her what had occurred up to this point. She issued a 72-hour hold on the suspect and ordered he be mentally evaluated at the Alaska Psychiatric Institute (API) in Anchorage.

Trooper Bayes and I had lunch, and then he transported me back to the airport, where I caught an airplane back to Seldovia.

Trooper Bayes and Trooper John Adams transported the suspect to API in Anchorage. The suspect underwent a mental evaluation and, in that he was now sober, he was found not to be suffering from a mental illness that would require he be confined, so he came back to Seldovia.

The suspect was summoned before the court on criminal mischief charges, relating to the damage to the jukebox at the Seldovia Lodge, and he pled guilty. He was given a fine and he had to pay the Lodge for the damage sustained to their machine. He was placed on one year's probation.

We would have many more contacts with this man. He had such a great personality, and was so likable when he was sober and not using any mind-altering drugs, but he fell into a deep depression, years after this incident, and, sadly, he wound up taking his own life. (Case Closed by Arrest and Mental Commitment)

Undercover Drug Operations

We called him N-261. He was a confidential informant (CI) for the Alaska State Troopers. Sgt. Gene Kallus of AST, the officer in charge of the AST South Central Area Narcotics Unit, (SCAN), out of the Soldotna Post, brought him to Seldovia, at my request. We were hopeful we could reduce a growing drug problem that was alleged to be taking place. We had numerous reports of marijuana, cocaine and some amphetamines that were alleged to be readily available. It was said to be an ever-growing problem. We had intelligence that named different local citizens who were said to be involved in the use and the distribution of these illicit drugs.

After becoming a member of SCAN, I was invited to take part in a number of undercover operations that took place in Anchorage and in the Matanuska Valley. I was sent to a marijuana eradication class in Palmer, Alaska. After the class was over, we raided a number of different grow operations in the Matanuska Valley. Search warrants were obtained, and a number of different teams stormed a number of grow operations simultaneously. Over 500 marijuana plants were confiscated, and a number of arrests were made.

I was also involved in a major statewide operation regarding cocaine and heroin, which were reportedly coming directly out of Mexico to Alaska. Surveillance was held on different locations all across the state, and a great deal of intelligence was gained. Search warrants were obtained, and simultaneously, raids were conducted on residences, office buildings, and warehouses all across the state. The statewide effort was a huge success, and a number of people were arrested and charged with several charges. Indictments were handed down, and many drug dealers lost their freedom due to the statewide sting operation. A lot of illegal drugs were seized, as well. The Department of Public Safety (DPS) reported the operation to be a huge success and promised to continue their efforts in the fight against all illicit drug activities in the state. Due to my involvement in SCAN, the Seldovia Police Department was able to get an undercover confidential informant sent to Seldovia. The state picked up all the expenses of the undercover operation, with the exception of the Seldovia police officer's wages. The CI was under my direction, and we were to work together to make buys of illicit drugs in and around Seldovia. N-261 had been working as a CI for the state for a long time and had been to Fairbanks, Nome, Wasilla, Palmer, Anchorage, Soldotna, and Homer before coming to Seldovia. He had bought a lot of drugs for AST and had made a lot of cases for the state. He was, however, hard to control. He had so much nervous energy, he was moving constantly, and I couldn't get much other police work done due to his need for constant contact with me. Maybe he had developed this condition due to all his undercover activity, always living on the edge. He was paranoid and always on edge. I certainly earned my wages while he was working for me.

I had never worked with a CI before, so I asked Sgt. Kallus to accompany me on our first controlled buy. The CI had set up a buy for the purchase of four, ¼ oz. baggies of marijuana from a local man. They had agreed on the price of $65 per gram, and the CI made arrangements to buy four baggies. The CI told the suspect he would be at his residence the following day at a given time. The CI set the time for the transaction for the next day to allow the police time to go before the court and apply for a glass warrant. A glass warrant is a search warrant for recording a verbal conversation between two parties. It is also called a wire warrant. After a CI has made a few buys, he establishes his credibility with the court, and his statements are then considered reliable. After a couple wire warrants are issued by the court, the process gets much easier.

The following day, at approximately 1845 hours, after having secured the wire warrant, Sgt. Kallus and I met with the CI at a predetermined location in a wooded area outside of town. Sgt. Kallus searched the CI's vehicle while I conducted a strip search of the CI. We had to be able to swear in a court of law that the CI did not have any contraband on his person, or accessible to him in his vehicle, at the time he purchased the drugs. After we had conducted the searches, the CI was given an electronic monitoring device, which was put on his person. With the device in place, the CI's conversations could be heard at all times, and the transaction could be recorded. I also gave the CI $270 in cash, which was to be used for the purchase of marijuana. I had previously photo-copied the money, in Sgt. Kallus' presence, prior to meeting with the CI.

We left the area of the meet, and Sgt. Kallus and I kept the CI in sight, and in audio contact, until he pulled into the suspect's driveway. Sgt. Kallus activated the recorder at that point to record the upcoming conversation. The CI made contact with the suspect inside the suspect's home, and the transaction was made. We could hear the conversation between the suspect and the CI. The CI was heard counting out the $260 he paid for the marijuana and he was heard asking the suspect if he could get him more marijuana. The suspect was heard telling him he'd have more later in the week. The CI left the residence and got back into his vehicle and backed out of the suspect's driveway. At this point, the recorder was turned off but the audio was left on so the CI could be monitored audibly. We again had him in sight and kept him in sight and sound back to the location of the meet outside of town.

After reaching the location of the meet, I again strip-searched the CI (I guess the rookie gets the dirty jobs), and Sgt. Kallus again searched the vehicle. I located a $10 bill in his shirt pocket, which I had given the CI to buy money prior to the transaction taking place. I retained the bill, but nothing else was found on his person. Sgt. Kallus located a brown paper bag containing four small foil-wrapped packages, each containing vegetable matter, in the front passenger's seat of the CI's vehicle. Nothing else was found in the vehicle.

Following the search of the CI and his vehicle, the CI was interviewed, and he reiterated what had taken place during the purchase of marijuana. He said the suspect, his wife, and two children, and another adult male, whom he called by name, were present at the time of the purchase, and all had witnessed the transaction. I was well acquainted with the man who the CI said was at the residence. He said the suspect got the marijuana out of the freezer portion of his refrigerator and he got the brown paper bag out of the trash and placed the four foil-wrapped packages inside. In his interview, the CI mentioned he had been strip-searched by me and his car had been searched by Sgt. Kallus prior to and following the purchase of the marijuana. Following the interview with the CI, we all left the location of the meet.

Sgt. Kallus and I went to the Seldovia PD where we field-tested the vegetable matter; the test showed a positive result for the presence of THC. The four foil packages were then put in a seal-a-meal plastic bag and logged into evidence, after having been packaged for shipment to the AST laboratory. The return report from the AST Lab listed four foil-wrapped small packages of vegetable matter weighing 6.8, 6.8, 6.7 and 6.7 grams, or a total of .058 pounds, and that they all tested positive for cannabis, marijuana. The foil packages further contained the fingerprints of our suspect, as was reported by the AST Lab.

This was my first undercover buy operation, and Sgt. Kallus described each step we took, telling me this is what is needed to successfully prosecute a drug case. I learned a lot and certainly would not have put this good of a case together had the Sergeant not been there. I found out how important it is to cross all your t's and dot all your i's.

Sgt. Kallus left after telling me no arrests would be made until the CI had completed all his work in Seldovia. He said we would then decide whether "Summons to Appear" or arrests would be conducted. He said Officer Lewis and I were now going to be on our own, running the local undercover operations. I just hoped I had learned enough to take over the helm. I was shocked by the amount of paperwork it takes to do an undercover buy. The paperwork takes nearly as long as it does to actually make the buy. When I was in Anchorage, assisting them in their operations, I never got involved in the paperwork end of things. Thank God! (Case Closed by Investigation)

Additional Undercover Drug Buys

I was again contacted by N-261, and he said he had another buy set up for the next day to purchase another ounce, 4 g, of marijuana, but this time from a different suspect. He told me the suspect's name, and I knew him quite well. I was given the particulars and I filled out the necessary paperwork for the wire warrant, as well as starting a file on this case. I called and made an appointment to go before our magistrate for a wire warrant. I responded to the courtroom and gave the application form to the magistrate. I was then sworn in and I reiterated what I had been told by the CI. The wire warrant was granted and I left the courtroom. I went to the police department and photocopied $260 in cash, which was to be used for the purchase of marijuana.

The following evening, I met with the CI at the prearranged time and I again strip-searched him and then I searched his vehicle. No contraband was found in either location. I then gave the CI the $260 I had photocopied, and then the electronic monitoring device was put on his person. We then left the area of the meet and headed into town. I kept the CI under visual and audio surveillance until he arrived at the suspect's residence. At this point, I activated the recorder to record any upcoming conversations. I observed him exit his vehicle and knock on the door of the camper trailer the suspect lived in. The door swung open, and he was invited in. I heard the conversation between the CI and the suspect. I heard the CI count out $260 and then ask if that was the amount agreed on. The suspect was heard to say it was correct. The suspect further told the CI that the marijuana he was buying was more of the same home-grown pot he'd purchased from our first suspect, who he called by name. The CI thanked him then and ask if there was any cocaine or anything else available in town. The suspect told him there was some coke around, but it was pretty hard to get ahold of. He told the CI he would have some more marijuana in a few days if the CI was interested. The CI told him he would be interested and he'd check back later. He then left the trailer and got back into his vehicle and left the residence. I shut off the recorder, left the monitor on and followed him back to the location of the meet. I kept the CI in both visual and audio surveillance all the way back to the location of the meet.

I again strip-searched the CI and then I searched his vehicle. Four small baggies of vegetable matter, believed to be marijuana, were found on his front seat packaged in four separate sandwich bags. No other contraband was found in his vehicle. The CI returned the electronic voice monitor, and I interviewed him. He, as he did in the previous case, outlined every step he'd taken in the purchase of the marijuana. He described the inside of the camper trailer and named an adult who was present and had witnessed the transaction. It was the same man who had been present at the previous residence when that purchase was made. This guy was becoming more and more interesting as the investigations continued.

The CI left the area of the meet, and I took the evidence to the office and logged it in as evidence. I field-tested the vegetable matter and got a positive reaction for the presence of THC. I then placed all four baggies in a seal-a-meal container and readied it for mailing to the AST Laboratory. The evidence was then stored in the evidence room.

The evidence was mailed to the AST Laboratory, and the vegetable matter was weighed and tested and found to be cannabis, marijuana. The plastic bags were examined for fingerprints, but no prints with sufficient ridge detail could be found.

The subject was later charged and pled guilty. He received jail time and lengthy probation. (Case Closed by Investigation)

Prior to the CI leaving Seldovia, we purchased marijuana on six more occasions, but the CI could not get into any cocaine or other drugs even though, he stated, they were present in town. In one of the cases, the CI made a buy of a five gallon bucket of marijuana for a total of $1600. Arrangements had been made for the CI to make four payments of $400 each per week, until he had it paid off. The marijuana had just been harvested and was being stored in a white five-gallon bucket. The marijuana was still green and would have to be dried before it could be used. The CI made all four payments, totaling $1600, and each time we had to go through the same routine we had gone through on the previous buys, which included getting a wire warrant for each of the installments. Each time he made a payment of $400, we had to go through the strip search, the automobile search, the monitoring of the transaction to and from the location of the payment, and the subsequent strip search, automobile search, and interview of the CI. It seemed as if we were either physically making a buy or I was sitting at my desk working on the mounds of paperwork, readying the cases for the district attorney. Each buy was its own case, and they were charged separately later in the year. The suspect who sold us the five pounds of marijuana was charged with four felony counts of distribution. The AST Lab weighed the vegetable matter in the five-gallon can, and it was reported to weigh 2,294 grams, or 5.57 pounds, and it tested positive as being cannabis, marijuana.

The district attorney bundled the four counts we had on the sale of the five pounds of marijuana, and the suspect pled Guilty on one (1) count. All four counts were used for sentencing purposes, and the suspect spent a great deal of time behind bars. The Alaska State Troopers took over the cases, and I never received the actual "Sentencing Reports," but I was told each of our suspects did plead guilty and serve jail time on the charges. I was not sad to see N-261, the CI, leave on the state ferry.

I did learn a lot during those undercover buys, and I learned how difficult it is to control a confidential informant. The undercover operation did surprise a lot of people, and I want to think we did some good for our community. Honestly, I was glad to see it end. I certainly wouldn't want to have to do this kind of operation every day, all year long. (Cases Closed by Investigation)

1983: A BUSY YEAR

The undercover drug operation lasted two months and took up a lot of my time. Officer Lewis was involved in some of the cases as well, but just because we were conducting undercover operations, all the other activity didn't slow down and had to be handled by the officers of the Seldovia Police Department. Jim Standefer, a dear friend and school teacher, volunteered to assist the department if we found ourselves in need of help. With the undercover operation taking up most of my time, we did bring Mr. Standefer on, and he was sworn in as a third officer in the Seldovia Police Department. Officer Standefer was a great choice as an alternate officer because he was very intelligent, thought things through before making a critical decision, knew how to handle himself, and was dearly loved by all who knew him.

To better understand why a third officer may be needed you should know that, along with the two months of undercover drug investigations, we were also investigating a number of other cases that year. We had one resisting arrest, one contributing to the delinquency of a minor case, three criminal mischief investigations, three minors charged with minor consuming alcohol, two charges were brought for furnishing liquor to minors, we took six theft reports, four burglaries of residences were investigated, six DWIs were charged, five negligent driving reports were followed up, one person was charged with shoplifting, two bad check cases were investigated, four vehicle accidents and two aircraft accidents were investigated, four criminal trespass cases were reported, two assaults were charged, one disorderly conduct was dealt with, two fraud cases were referred to the district attorney, one suicide threat was handled, there was one investigation of a burglary of a business, we responded to two domestic disturbances, one search & rescue took place and we investigated one homicide. I know I keep reiterating but, the traffic control and patrol, the bar checks, the citizens needing assistance, and the unending paperwork still goes on regardless.

SEARCH AND RESCUE

It was 0520 hours on June 21, 1983, when I was awakened by a loud knocking on the door of my residence. I got up, threw on a pair of sweat pants, and hurried to answer the door. The man standing at my doorway was a fisherman and he told me he needed to talk to me about a man who was left on Gore Point out of Port Dick the previous morning. I invited the man·in and put a pot of water on to boil for coffee. We took a seat at the kitchen table, and the man told me he was a halibut fisherman and had hired a crew of two to deckhand for him for the 12-hour season opener the Fish & Game had scheduled. He said the crew did fine on the way to Port Dick and they had baited all the hooks and got everything ready to set when the season opened. He said they reached Port Dick early and had around three hours before they could set any gear, so they anchored up, and the crew was catching a couple hours sleep. He said he awoke to a noise out on deck. When he got up to see what the noise was, he observed one deckhand throwing gear around, some of which went overboard, and he said the guy was freaking out. He grabbed him and after the other crewmember woke up, he aided in restraining the man. The captain said the deckhand continued to struggle so they had no choice but to put him ashore on Gore Point with his duffle bag. He said he told the man to stay put and he'd come back and pick him up after the season closed in another thirteen hours. He said they left the man food and, after the season closed, they went back to pick the guy up,

131

but he was nowhere to be found. Not knowing really what to do, the skipper said he headed for town to report the incident to the police. He said he left Gore Point and came directly to Seldovia and wasted no time before coming to my house.

I took the skipper's name and his personal information, as well as his other deckhand's, and the name of the man he'd left on Gore Point. We had a cup of coffee, and he then left to continue his trip to Homer, where he could deliver his fish. I told him we'd call the troopers and take care of the problem.

As soon as he left, I called Trooper Bayes and woke him up. I relayed what the man had told me, and Trooper Bayes directed me to call and make arrangements to fly the area so we could search for the guy. I told him it was raining, with a low ceiling, but I'd make the call and set everything up in hopes we could fly. He told me to tell the pilot it would be a search & rescue, and the state would supply a purchase order number, which they would need for billing purposes.

Jack Hein, a good friend and a great pilot, lived in Seldovia. He worked for Cook Inlet Aviation, so I called him at home and woke him up. I told him we needed to fly a search & rescue in the area of Gore Point at Port Dick and I gave him what information I had. Jack said he'd have to go to Homer first to fuel up but he could fly Trooper Bayes and me in their Cessna 172. I ask what time he'd want Trooper Bayes to be at the airport, and he said we could probably get underway out of Homer around 0630 hours. I told him I'd tell Trooper Bayes. I told him I'd head out to the Seldovia Airport around 0645 hours so I would be there when they stopped to pick me up.

Just prior to 0700 hours, Jack and Trooper Bayes arrived at the airport, and I climbed into the seat behind the pilot. It was still raining lightly, with a low ceiling, and Jack told me we would have to go down around the end of the Peninsula instead of cutting across land, making our trip considerably longer. We took off and flew south over English Bay and continued on through Chugach Pass. We then turned toward the northeast and flew to Port Dick, which is located on the Gulf of Alaska. Gore Point, where the man was alleged to have been set ashore, was located on the north side of Port Dick.

Jack flew us down the beach from Gore Point, into the small bay to the north, after entering Port Dick. We had not seen anyone thus far and we were told the man was wearing yellow rain gear. He should have been rather easy to spot, wearing such bright colors. We continued to fly to the north, through the bite, and into Nuka Bay. We flew out around Gore Point, on the Nuka Bay side, and then, again, followed the beach down and into Port Dick from Gore Point. We still didn't see any sign of life. Jack flew across the small bay this time and then swung to the north, searching the other side of the bay. Jack sighted the man first and, after flying past him, turned the plane around to fly by him again. Jack told me he would keep the man visible on the left side of the aircraft, and he'd open his door window and throttle back on the airplane when we got alongside the man, and that I was to yell for him to stay put. Jack said we'd have to go back to Homer and get a floatplane to pick the man up. Jack flew by the man with his window open and, when he chopped the throttle of the airplane, I yelled, "Stay put," to the guy. I'm pretty sure he heard me. On this pass, we saw where the man had tied two long logs together, which, we assumed, he'd used to row across the mouth of the small bay. His duffle bag was also seen on the beach beside him.

The rain had subsided, but the clouds were still very low, and we, again, had to fly around the south end of the peninsula and back up Kachemak Bay, to get to Homer. It took us nearly an hour to reach Homer. Jack taxied up to the Cook Inlet office, and we went inside, where Jack called Bill DeCreft of Kachemak Airlines and asked if he'd be available to fly to Port Dick on a search & rescue for the troopers. He told Mr. DeCreft we'd already located a man who needed to be picked up and brought to Homer. Mr. DeCreft told Jack his son would fly us in his single-engine Otter. He said his son would meet us at his airplane in half an hour.

When we arrived at the floatplane, Jose' DeCreft was already warming up the engine. Jack Hein wanted to accompany us on the flight and, since space was not an issue, Trooper Bayes told him he didn't see a problem. After we were all aboard and buckled in, we took off. Jack Hein sat in the co-pilot's seat with Trooper Bayes and me setting in the second row. The clouds had lifted somewhat, and we were able to fly overland to Port Dick, making the trip a lot shorter than going around the south end of the peninsula. As we entered Port Dick, you could see the white caps on the water, which was created by the northeast wind which had started to blow. When Jose' landed in the small bay, where the subject was stranded, he had to taxi up close to the beach and then turn the nose of the aircraft offshore, into the wind, and let the wind push the aircraft back onto the beach, with the tail of the airplane toward the beach. As soon as the floats were on the beach, Trooper Bayes exited and assisted the stranded deckhand on board. Jose' again started the floatplane, and we taxied out, away from the beach, and took off in a northeasterly direction, into the wind.

Trooper Bayes had prepared a thermos of coffee he'd brought with us, as well as a couple sandwiches, and he offered the deckhand both the coffee and the sandwiches. The deckhand refused both, stating he was fine. He said he was going to walk to Seldovia and said he could have made it without any assistance. He was totally soaked to the bone, and all his belongings, in the duffle bag, were also wet. We were again able to fly across the landmass and after we landed in Homer, we all exited the airplane. Trooper Bayes, the deckhand, and I left in the trooper's patrol vehicle. We drove to the AST office, which they shared with Homer PD. Trooper Bayes then interviewed the deckhand. He said his skipper put him off on the beach following an argument, and he decided not to wait for him, and to walk to Seldovia. He denied throwing the fishing gear overboard. He did say he had rowed across the small bay after tying two logs together with some rope he had with him. He said he used a board he'd found to row with.

The man was nearly hypothermic and was shaking and shivering. Following the interview, he asked Trooper Bayes where the nearest laundromat was located, because he wanted to dry all his clothes. The trooper told him it was approximately two blocks away. The man then asked the trooper if he would give him a ride because he didn't know if he could walk that far. The trooper chuckled and then asked him, "And you were going to walk to Seldovia from Port Dick?" The man didn't say anything more. He just picked up his duffle bag and walked out of the police department, not to be seen again by either the trooper or by me.

It was very clear to both myself and the trooper that the deckhand would have died if we had not responded and picked him up. He was totally soaked, as were all his clothes, and he had a long way to go before he could even start to walk to Seldovia. He still had another bay to row across, which was much larger than the one he'd made it across, and then he had to go up the West Arm of Port Dick, and then cross overland through the Rocky River area to access the road that leads out from the Gulf side. He would certainly have died but for his being rescued. (Case Closed, Subject Rescued)

MY FIRST HOMICIDE INVESTIGATION

At approximately 0002 hours on May 25, 1983, I received a telephone call reporting that a stabbing had occurred on Shoreline Drive. I quickly dressed and responded to the scene. Upon arrival, I observed a vehicle that belonged to a local man who was on the scene. It was parked just off the roadway. I observed the doctor and three other people present. The ambulance was on scene; its back doors were open and a gurney was setting just behind the vehicle.

The victim was lying beside the roadway, with no shirt on, and I observed, what appeared to be, a knife wound in his left chest area. I asked the doctor what had happened, and he told me the young man with the vehicle, which was parked just off the roadway, had gotten into a physical altercation with the victim, and a knife came into play, and the victim was stabbed. The doctor said they were going to medivac the victim to Homer Hospital. He said he would, most probably, have to undergo an operation. The EMTs were present with the ambulance and were readying the victim for transport.

I asked the suspect to have a seat in my patrol vehicle. I read him his Miranda warning, and he agreed to talk to me. I activated a voice recorder and advised him he was being recorded. In the interview, he admitted to stabbing the victim, stating that the victim had attacked him, and he was afraid of him, and thought he was going to be seriously injured. He said the knife was in the console, between the front seats, inside his vehicle and, when the victim was attempting to pull him out of his vehicle, he grabbed the knife, unfolded the blade, and showed it to the victim, in hopes it would discourage any further attacks. He said the victim lunged forward and wound up falling onto the knife. He said the victim was very intoxicated and had him stop the vehicle as he was walking up Shoreline Drive. The suspect said the victim opened the door on the driver's side of his vehicle and attacked him. He reiterated that he had no intention of stabbing him and that the victim fell onto the blade of the knife.

Following the initial interview with the suspect, I released him and told him to meet me at the Seldovia Police Department. I checked with the doctor and asked if I would be needed at the scene; he told me they had the victim ready to be medevac'd and they would transport him to the airport, where they would wait on the airplane. I left the scene and went to the Seldovia PD. I asked the suspect to wait in his vehicle while I made a call to Trooper Bayes of the Alaska State Troopers. I woke the trooper up and I told him what had happened and asked him, since I didn't have a jail, what I should do with the suspect. I told him I felt I had a felony assault. I was advised to get a very thorough interview, then release the suspect, and tell him not to leave town. The Trooper told me to keep him advised on the case's progress.

I had the suspect come into the office and I again interviewed him, after again reading him his Miranda warning. On this occasion, I had him sign a "Waiver of Rights" form. He basically told me the same story he had told me before but added that he and the victim had been in two previous altercations that evening. He said the victim was very intoxicated and was the aggressor. Following the interview, I released the suspect and told him to stick around town. He assured me he wasn't going anywhere.

I went home and went back to bed, only to be awakened at approximately 0430 hours by the doctor. He told me the victim had died as a result of the knife wound. He said, "You now have a homicide." I had never worked a homicide before and I was really concerned. I knew I'd need help with this one. I called Trooper Bayes and woke him for the second time that night. After I told him the victim had succumbed as a result of the stabbing, the trooper told me to go to the scene, secure it with police tape, and keep everyone away. He said I should post an officer there to see that no one entered the scene. He told me to block the road and not to allow any traffic to pass. He said he would catch the first available airplane and would come to town to assist me in the investigation.

After I got off the phone with Trooper Bayes, I called Officer Lewis, who was on his day off, and requested he gear up and meet me at the scene. I responded to the scene; I taped it off and closed the road. Officer Lewis showed up, and I told him to stay on the scene and not let anyone into the area, which included any vehicular traffic.

I picked up Trooper Bayes at the airport, and we discussed the case, and what our next move would be. It was decided we would first work the scene of the homicide and then we'd re-interview the suspect. We responded to the crime scene, and drawings, with measurements, were made. When I had interviewed the suspect, he told me he'd thrown the knife over the bank, and upon searching for it, we located it on the beach below the scene of the crime. A small amount of blood was visible on the blade of the knife. The blade was still open on the knife and hadn't been folded shut. A series of photographs were taken, and then the police tape was taken down, and the road was opened.

We responded to the police department and, at Trooper Bayes' suggestion, I called the suspect and told him we needed to re-interview him. Since he lived out of town, he told me it'd be a little bit before he could get to the PD. When he did arrive, his father was with him.

I introduced the suspect and his father to Trooper Bayes. The trooper shook hands with both parties and then told the suspect he needed to interview him again, since the victim had succumbed due to the injuries sustained in the altercation. The suspect said he understood, and the trooper read him his Miranda rights again, and had him sign the rights form. He said he understood his rights and agreed to talk to us. Basically, the suspect told the trooper the same thing he'd told me, but the trooper did expound in some areas. Following the interview, Trooper Bayes told the suspect he was under arrest for murder in the second degree and he told him he would have to go with him to Homer. Trooper Bayes explained to the suspect and his father that he would be arraigned in Homer Court, and bail would be set. The amount of the bail would be determined by the presiding judge, and the suspect would be given a public defender if it was determined he could not afford a lawyer, as was stated in the Miranda warning. As he placed the suspect in handcuffs, the trooper asked that I call and make arrangements for an airplane. The suspect was handcuffed in front and told he'd have to be handcuffed when being transported, as is the policy of the Alaska State Troopers. Trooper Bayes told the suspect's father that the vehicle in which the altercation occurred would have to be impounded and that I would be taking care of that. The suspect told us the vehicle was parked in his father's driveway and the keys were in the ignition.

I transported the trooper and the suspect to the airport, and the suspect's father drove to the airport as well, to say goodbye to his son. I called Officer Lewis and told him I'd be by to pick him up. I picked him up and we went to the suspect's father's residence to pick up the suspect's vehicle. Officer Lewis drove the vehicle to the city impound yard, where an inventory was done, after which it was locked up.

A Grand Jury was called, and they come back with a True Bill, charging the suspect with murder in the second degree. At the arraignment, the defendant pled not guilty and the court set a jury trial date. Bail was set at $10,000 cash, or corporate bond, and a third party custodian was ordered. The defendant was further ordered not to use drugs or drink any alcoholic beverages and he was ordered not to leave the Third Judicial District without first obtaining permission from the court.

A $10,000 corporate bond usually involves a jail bondsman, who carries the bond with the court. The suspect has to come up with 10 percent of the bond amount, so in this case he would have to come up with $1,000. A third-party custodian is a person who agrees to keep the suspect in sight or sound 24 hours per day, seven days per week. The third-party custodian has to be authorized by the court, so they have to go before the judge and answer a series of questions under oath. The judge explains to them that they can be charged with a crime and held accountable if they fail to keep the defendant in view 24/7.

They also are responsible for seeing to it that the defendant abides by all the conditions of release the judge has ordered. Again, if they fail in any part of their responsibility, and the defendant breaks the rules, the suspect can be arrested, and the third party custodian can also be brought before the court on charges.

As in most serious cases, this case dragged on for months. The defendant did make bail, and his father was appointed as his third party custodian. The case finally ended with a plea bargain between the district attorney's office and the defendant's attorney. The charges were reduced from murder in the second degree to criminal negligent homicide, which held a maximum sentence of five years in prison. The defendant, after changing his plea to guilty of criminal negligent homicide was given a sentence of two years in jail on the charge of criminal negligent homicide and another one-year sentence in Jail for violating his probation stemming from a previous felony conviction. In total, the defendant was sentenced to three years in prison, and was given a probation period of ten years upon getting out of jail. He would then start his ten years of probation, where he had to keep in monthly contact with his probation officer.

I felt, in this case, justice was served, in that we really don't know what actually happened in the confrontation between the two young men. The case had a great impact here in Seldovia, as both of the boys were born and raised here. They were both best friends, nearly the same age, who had grown up together. Alcohol played a big part in this case, and the two were in a confrontation over a girlfriend. Everyone lost in this case. There were no winners. (Case Closed by Arrest)

A DRIVING WHILE INTOXICATED REPORT AND INVESTIGATION

On September 11, 1983, at approximately 0015 hours, my wife observed a green Volkswagen drive across the yard located on the corner of Alder Street and Harborview Drive. Since I was out of town at the time, she called the on-duty officer, Jim Standefer, by radio, and reported the incident.

Jim was a school teacher who assisted the police department in the summers when we were shorthanded. He was a great choice as a police officer; he was very intelligent and had common sense, which is very important for a police position, and he was well-liked by everyone in the community.

After receiving the radio call from Ann, Officer Standefer located the subject on the waterside of the residence located at 251 Main Street. The vehicle was observed by the officer to leave the area and drive over a curb to gain access to Main Street. The vehicle swerved back and forth on the roadway and then made an abrupt left turn into the Linwood Bar parking lot. Officer Standefer blocked any exit by pulling up behind the subject's vehicle with the patrol vehicle. The officer then exited his patrol vehicle and approached the subject. When the suspect saw the officer approaching, he took the keys out of the ignition of the Volkswagen and threw them on the floorboard of the vehicle. He then stated, "I wasn't driving. I wasn't driving." Officer Standefer directed the suspect to exit the vehicle. Upon exiting, the suspect staggered and had to grab the vehicle to keep from falling. When asked to produce an operator's license, he told the officer he didn't have one. When asked how much alcohol he'd drunk, the suspect stated he had consumed one beer. Officer Standefer then transported the suspect to the Seldovia Police Department, where he asked him to perform some field sobriety tests. When asked to do the heel to toe test and, after Officer Standefer showed him what was expected, the suspect attempted the test and staggered into the desk, nearly falling down. He was then directed to touch the tip of his nose with the finger of his right hand. He attempted this test but was unable to complete it satisfactorily. When Officer Standefer started to explain another test, the suspect flipped him off and swore at the officer, refusing to do any further tests.

Officer Standefer called Bob Gruber and made arrangements to fly the suspect to Homer, so a breathalyzer test could be conducted, and an officer trained in DWI arrests could take over the case. Officer Standefer had accompanied me on a number of DWI arrests and knew the basics but was not trained in the breathalyzer or the paperwork needed to complete the case.

The suspect was handcuffed and transported to Homer via Cook Inlet Aviation, and Officer William Geragotelis of the Homer Police Department met the airplane. Officer Standefer and the suspect were transported to the Homer Police Department. Officer Geragotelis had the suspect perform a series of field sobriety tests while being video-taped. The suspect was given his rights to an independent test, and he requested a blood sample be drawn. Officer Geragotelis transported the suspect to the Homer Hospital, and blood was drawn and sealed for evidentiary purposes. Upon returning to the Homer Police Department, Officer Geragotelis gave the suspect a breathalyzer test with a result of 0.26 percent blood alcohol. The officer then read the suspect his Miranda warning, and the suspect agreed to be interviewed. Following the suspect signing the waiver, Officer Geragotelis interviewed him. After it was daylight, Officer Standefer was transported back to the Homer Airport, where he caught a flight back to Seldovia. He carried with him a copy of the paperwork Officer Geragotelis had filled out as well as the blood that was taken from the suspect at the Homer Hospital. Upon reaching the Seldovia Police Department, Officer Standefer locked the blood evidence in the refrigerator to preserve it until it could be sent to the AST Laboratory.

I returned home later in the day, and Officer Standefer and I discussed the case. I was very pleased with how the officer had handled the case, and the end result was that the suspect wound up pleading No Contest to the charge of DWI and was sentenced by the court.

The blood evidence was packaged and sent to the AST Laboratory. It confirmed the breathalyzer report with a similar finding of 0.26% blood alcohol.

When the suspect was being held in Homer Jail, his live-in girlfriend came to the police department and told me she was in fear the suspect would be angry when he got out of jail, and he might assault her or her children. She asked if there was any way to keep him locked up. I told her she could request a restraining order from the court, if she feared for her safety, and she could show the court why she had these concerns. I told her he legally could not return to the residence without a police escort if the restraining order was issued. She asked if he could be sentenced to a longer time in jail. I told her the first time DWI only carries three days in jail as it was then mandated by the Alaska Statutes. She asked if I would deliver a letter to the court before the suspect was arraigned, and I told her I could fax it over if she wanted me to. She sat down at the police department and wrote the judge a letter, which I faxed over to the court. The letter included her contact information. However, I never learned if a restraining order was issued.

The suspect was sentenced to thirty days in jail with all but 72 hours suspended. He was given a $250 fine, was placed on probation for one year, and ordered not to drive until he had a valid operator license.

The Seldovia Police Department wasn't called for any domestic problems at the suspect's residence after his return home. We had put the residence on the hot list for frequent patrols but, thank goodness, nothing happened.

Officer Bill Geragotelis was another officer who was a great asset to the Seldovia Police Department on a number of different occasions.

He was a good officer and a great resource for the Seldovia Police Department, and a man who I am proud to call a friend. (Case Closed by Arrest).

SUICIDE THREAT

On December 22, 1983, at approximately 2045 hours, a citizen called the Seldovia Police Department and reported that he had just received a call from a local woman, whom he named, who told him she had a pistol in her mouth, and that she was going to kill herself. The caller said the police needed to get to her residence quickly.

Both Officer Lewis and I were at the department at the time and we both responded in my police vehicle. The lady's residence was only a couple blocks from the department, and we got there very quickly. Upon arrival, we found the entry door to be ajar and open approximately four inches. I called out to the lady, calling her by name and announcing ourselves as police officers. I then pushed the door wide open. I observed the lady to be sitting on her couch; she was holding a plastic bag. I walked directly up to her and I then observed that there were bullets in the plastic sandwich bag. It was very apparent to both Officer Lewis and me that the lady was highly intoxicated. I ask her where the gun was, and she said, "What gun?" She then said it was under the couch and she started to reach for it, but I grabbed her arm and told her I'd get it. I reached under the couch and pulled out a .22 caliber pistol. I then asked if she was going to kill herself. She said yes, but said the bullets would not fit into the gun. She was tired of everything, she stated.

I secured the .22 caliber pistol and took the bullets from her, which she had in the bag. The bullets were .38 caliber, thus the reason for them not fitting in the .22 caliber pistol. I told the lady she was going to have to come with us, and she asked if she was under arrest. I told her she was but it was for protective custody and she wasn't being charged with any crime. She left with us without any problems. We took the pistol and the bullets to put them in safekeeping.

After we arrived at the police department, I called the doctor and asked if he would come to the department. I told him what was going on and I told him I wanted the lady medically evaluated. I also wanted his professional opinion as to how serious she was about killing herself.

The doctor arrived and he conducted an evaluation. He talked to her for quite a while before he came to me and told me that she needed to be watched throughout the night and given a chance to sober up. He said she should be flown out somewhere the next day for a mental evaluation. He suggested Homer Mental Health, and I told him I'd see what I could do. I asked that he put his opinion in writing, so, if I had to go before the court for a court order, I could use his letter along with a "Police Mental Commitment Form." I provided the paper, and the doctor wrote out a note outlining his observations and his thoughts regarding the lady being evaluated.

I talked to the lady and told her we had to make some decisions. Since we didn't have a jail facility, and since she had to be watched all night, we could do one of two things. I could hire a female guard to sit with her at her home or, if she didn't want to do that, she would have to spend the night on a cot here at the police department. As I was hoping, she said she wanted to spend the night at her own home. I told her that is what we would do then, but I informed her that this was not over. I told her I'd be picking her up the next morning, and we'd be flying to Homer so she could talk to a professional about how she has been feeling. She was not at all in favor of that, but I told her we'd discuss that later. I then called a lady friend and told her I needed someone to sit with the lady that night to see that she didn't harm herself. The lady friend agreed to sit with her and she said she would be at the Seldovia Police Department in a few minutes. After my friend arrived, I delivered the lady back to her apartment, and arrangements were made for the night. I told my friend she would have to be awake all night to ensure no harm came to the lady. She agreed, and I left the apartment.

The next morning, I made arrangements for the lady and me to travel to Homer. She was sober now, and I told her she needed to be evaluated and that she had to make another choice. She could either agree and willingly go to be evaluated, or I could go before the court and apply for a court order. She agreed to voluntarily be evaluated, and we flew to Homer. I made arrangements for the lady to get a return ticket on the airlines and, after delivering her to Homer Mental Health's office, I went to the airport and flew back home.

I'm pleased to announce the lady did get the help she needed and she lived a very happy life for many more years.

In my nearly 32-year career, the cases that meant the most to me were the ones where I could actually assist someone in a positive way and then, later on, see the fruits of my labor. It is rare, but I've had people come to me after a few years of my having been involved in their lives, and thank me for my services, telling me it changed their lives. It doesn't get any better than that. (Case Closed – Protective Custody)

1984: A BUSY YEAR

In 1984, it was business as usual at the Seldovia Police Department. We continued to investigate some cases from 1983, and the calls continued coming in. In 1984, we had a report of a person possessing illegal king crab, one minor was charged with minor possessing alcohol, one adult was charged with furnishing liquor to minors, an adult went before the court on charges of misconduct involving weapons, there were three automobile accidents investigated, one aircraft accident occurred, there were five DWI's, one refusal to submit to breath test, one missing person report which involved a joint search involving the Alaska State Troopers, the Alaska Parks Mountain Rescue Team, and the Seldovia Police Department. Police responded to one suicide attempt, three thefts were reported, one report was taken for property damage, two persons were cited for driving with license revoked, one criminal trespass was reported, three people were charged with disorderly conduct, three death investigations were conducted, police responded to one suspicious circumstance call, one person was charged with reckless driving, while another man was charged with negligent driving, two reports were taken for criminal mischief, one assault was investigated. The Seldovia Police Department assisted another agency in the investigation of a report of sexual assault of a minor, police and fire responded to one fire report up in Seldovia Bay, a marijuana grow operation was taken down and one person was charged with misconduct involving drugs in the 6th degree, and one warrant arrest was made of a local man for failure to appear at his court hearing. Patrolling, traffic control, and public assists continued, making 1984 a very busy year. A death in the family took me out of state for a month and Officer Jerry Lewis, with the assistance of Officer John Gruber, covered the department in my absence.

A huge change occurred in the Seldovia Police Department in 1984 when, in early fall, we moved into our new police department, which had been under construction during the summer months. The department was built following the guidelines Captain C.E. Swackhammer, Swack, had suggested, so we could hopefully obtain a jail contract with DPS sometime down the road.

The facility had two jail cells with a bunk bed in each cell, making it possible to house four prisoners at a time, if needed. The cells also had the stainless-steel sink/commode combination, as per Swack's suggestion, and a sprinkler system, for fire suppression, was installed. Both cells were plumbed with circulating air that could be enhanced by an exhaust fan system. The facility had a booking area and an evidence room. An outer office and an inner office gave both the patrol officer and me our own office space. The entry door faced to the east, and there was a door that also led to the newly constructed fire department.

The fire department was also built during the summer of 1984 and was a two-bay facility with a loft for storage, a small office, and an area for rollout gear to be stored. The firetruck and the ambulance could now be housed in the fire department, freeing up space in the city shop for the maintenance crew's use. Things were looking up for the emergency responders in Seldovia. The fire department grew in number; some new people studied, passed their EMT exams, and became first responders, as well. Now it was going to be much easier for both the fire/EMT personnel, and the officers of the police department to conduct business in a more confidential and professional manner. Everyone was excited about the future in our new facilities.

MISSING PERSON

Sometime in late June of 1984, the Alaska State Troopers started a search for a young lady, twenty-one years of age, who was reportedly missing out of Homer. The girl's mother had called from California and told the Homer Police dispatcher that her daughter was on a trip to Alaska. The mother said the girl was a free spirit who liked the wilderness; she had made plans to go into the back country and live off the land for the summer. She told her mother she would call her before she started her trek. She had also told her mother she was considering Seldovia or Kodiak. The last communication with her daughter was two weeks ago, the mother said. She also said her daughter usually called a couple times a week and she was getting very worried.

The Homer Police Department contacted the Alaska Ferry Terminal in Homer and asked that they check their records to see if the girl had purchased a ticket to either Seldovia or to Kodiak. The records were checked, and no one with that name could be found in their system either to Seldovia or Kodiak.

The search was continued throughout the summer months, with the girl's mother calling Homer police dispatch every few days. The Alaska State Troopers called me and gave me a description of the girl and asked that I check around to see if she might have come to Seldovia on a private boat or an airplane. I called the airlines serving Seldovia and had them check their records, but both could not find anyone with her name flying with them. I asked around and couldn't find anyone who remembered anyone meeting the girl's description. There were no breaks in the case until, at approximately 1350 hours on November 24, I received a call from a lady who summers in Seldovia with her husband. She said she had seen a missing person's flyer on the missing girl and she wanted the police to know that she'd met the girl in Homer on May 25, when she was waiting to board the state ferry, Tustumena, to Seldovia. She said the girl traveled to Seldovia with her and her husband and she helped them unload their vehicle at their residence. She further said that the girl told her she needed some time alone and was going to check out the Jakolof Bay area for a couple weeks to a month. She was reported to be in good spirits and was looking forward to her upcoming adventure. She turned down a ride to the Jakolof area from the lady. She promised to stop by for coffee when she came back through Seldovia on her way to the States in the fall, the lady reported. They said that was the last time they saw the girl.

The husband of the lady who called told me that he had spent much more time with the missing girl than his wife had. He said she was wearing army fatigue trousers, hiking boots, a plaid shirt, and silver-rimmed glasses. She had also told him she needed some time to herself. He said she told him she was going to the Jakolof Bay or Rocky River areas. He reported she had a lot of visquine she would use to make a shelter. She had dirty blonde hair that was worn in a ponytail and she was a girl of a large built, he said.

I contacted the Alaska State Troopers and told them about the new information, then I called the Alaska State Ferry Terminal in Homer and gave them the dates the girl was alleged to have been traveling with them. When they checked that date, they did find she had traveled to Seldovia from Homer and they apologized for not locating it the first time.

The flyer of the missing girl was sent to me, and I made copies and spread it all around Seldovia, hoping someone had seen the girl. On November 25, at approximately 1950 hours, a man who lives in the outer area of town reported that he had just seen the flyer on the missing girl and he wanted to report that he had taken her to the bottom of the switchbacks, at the head of Jakolof Bay. He said she had told him she was going to the headwaters of Rocky River, where she would set up a camp. He reported she was set up very well for a stay in the wilderness, and that she was in good spirits, and looking forward to her upcoming adventure. He said she told him she had been in the area for two days, on a previous occasion, and she wanted to spend the next two months exploring the area. He said she was wearing a plaid shirt, blue jeans, a dark coat, and was carrying a large backpack that was dark in color. She was reportedly wearing thick glasses with wire rims, which would be indicative of someone who has vision problems. She told him she was a student in a college somewhere in the States, and that she was on her summer break, and needed to get some time alone.

With the new information, Daniel Weatherby of the Alaska State Troopers requested the AST helicopter for a search & rescue mission. The AST Helicopter pilot, Robert Larson, Trooper Weatherly and I flew for over two hours and searched the Rocky River, Red Mountain, and Barbary Creek areas with no sightings of the missing girl.

The Alaska State Troopers, knowing the missing girl was in the Red Mountain/Rocky River area according to the last reports, brought in a mountain rescue team. The team consisted of nine people. They started their search on July 20, 1985. In parties of three, they searched the Rocky River area from the headwaters to the ocean. They also searched the Red Mountain area, including the area of the mine shaft at an elevation of 3,000 feet. In addition, they searched the Jakolof Bay area, which included searching the trail to the Tutka Bay Lagoon. The searchers focused on areas that were likely to be used by someone carrying a heavy pack, and needing to replenish water supplies. The search lasted a total of four days. No sightings were made of the missing girl or a campsite she may have used.

With the girl having been missing for over a year, everyone had lost hope that she was still alive. She could have gotten transportation back to Homer on a boat out of Jakolof Bay Harbor but, if that were true, she most probably would have contacted her family, and they had not heard from her. Now a second winter would be here soon, and the missing girl was not equipped to spend one winter in the wilderness, let alone two.

On August 1, 1985, a year and a half since the girl was reported missing, I received a call from a man who told me he'd gone into Jakolof Bay with his family on his boat to dig some butter clams. He said he had a wife and three small children, and he had breached his boat on the northeast beach across Jakolof Bay from the harbor facility. After beaching the boat, he said he had to go to the bathroom, so he walked up into the wooded area out of sight of his family. He said something blue in color, at the base of a tree, caught his attention. Upon closer inspection, he said he observed a blue sleeping bag with a skull lying at the head of it. He said he immediately left without touching anything; he loaded up his family and went to find a phone to call the police. I took the man's personal information and told him the Alaska State Troopers would likely want to speak with him at a later date. I thanked the man for the information and then terminated the phone call.

I immediately called Trooper Dan Weatherly at the Homer Post of AST and told him of the report. The trooper asked me if I knew where the man was talking about, and I told him I did. It was the only sandy beach area visible from the Jakolof Bay Harbor facility and it was across the bay in a northeasterly direction. Trooper Weatherly told me he would bring the trooper's Boston Whaler and he would meet me at the Jakolof Bay Harbor, and we could go to the location together. He said he'd bring Trooper John Adams with him. I left Seldovia within half an hour and drove the 10 miles to the Jakolof Bay Harbor. Troopers Weatherly and Adams arrived, and I boarded the Boston Whaler, and we went across Jakolof Bay to the described location.

We walked into the wooded area and observed the blue sleeping bag right away. Upon closer examination, we found the skull that had been reported and other bones that were strewn around the area. A backpack, some clothing items, and personal items were also observed in the general area. Prior to gathering any evidence, photographs were taken of the scene. After photographing the area, we searched the general area for other evidence. Numerous human bones were found in the area surrounding the sleeping bag, and it was evident animals had strewn the bones around. A billfold was found with the missing girl's driver's license and other means of identification. The location of each bone was measured and logged. Two journals were found near the remains, and there were numerous entries in each book. One of the journals was a medical journal, where the girl had logged her medical problems. She evidently had a lot of female problems, and this was what was written about most in the journal. In the other journal was a daily log, which had pages and pages of entries. As we reviewed the entries, it became evident that the young lady was becoming more and more distraught as time went on. She referenced the boats going up and down the bay and she wrote she would yell out to them, telling them, "Can't you see what you're doing to the environment?" She had another entry where she said she walked out from her camp into a place where she thought no man had ever trod, and what does she run into but a power line. She wrote how she clawed her way to the top of the mountain and yelled at the top of her voice, "Can't you see what you're doing to the environment?" There was an entry that she had spent three days in her sleeping bag, retching and vomiting, after she had eaten some roots of a plant that must have poisoned her. She complained about having no fresh water to drink; she had camped in an area that was close to salt water, but there was no fresh water anywhere nearby. She had written that although she knew it was bad for her, she had been drinking salt water and couldn't seem to stop. Most of the entries in the journal were about the different places she'd explored, the plants, and the scenery. It is evident to the reader that she was failing toward the last of her entries due to the change in her descriptions of the events she was writing about. Her last entry was on July 7, 1984.

Following the collection of the evidence, we packaged everything and loaded it in the Boston Whaler. The troopers dropped me off at the Jakolof Bay Harbor and they continued on their way to Homer. I drove into Seldovia and started putting on paper my report for the Alaska State Troopers.

The missing girl's parents were notified and given the sad news. At least they were able to bring their daughter home and bury her. I do hope they found some closure. (Case Closed – Located Remains)

MISCONDUCT INVOLVING WEAPONS, MINOR CONSUMING ALCOHOL, FURNISHING LIQUOR TO MINORS

On December 26, 1984, just prior to 0200 hours, I received a call from a lady who reported hearing a rifle shot followed by a woman's scream; she said it came from the residence next door to her residence. Directly after hearing the shot, she observed the shadow of someone run by her residence. The caller said she didn't know what was going on, but thought it couldn't be anything good.

I called Officer Lewis on the radio and conveyed the report to him. I was awakened by the call and, since he was on patrol, I told Officer Lewis I was getting ready to go, and for him to wait for me, and we'd both respond. I didn't want him responding alone to a call of this nature.

Officer Lewis and I arrived at the residence where the shot had reportedly been fired, and I knocked on the door. A lady answered the door, and we asked if we could come in and talk to her. From the doorway, I observed what appeared to be a .22 caliber rifle leaning against the wall and a large-bore rifle lying on the couch. She invited us in, and she said her boyfriend had gotten into a verbal altercation with a man who was visiting, and he had told the visitor to leave and, after the man went outside, her boyfriend grabbed a rifle and fired it into the air outside the home to make sure the guy left. She said her boyfriend had left after that but she didn't know where he'd gone. I asked her if she was home alone, and she said she was. I asked for permission to search the residence to make sure no one else was present, and she refused, saying no one else was there. It was apparent to both Officer Lewis and I that the lady was intoxicated. There were beer cans on the table and on the coffee table, which we assumed were empty, in that they had all been opened.

At that point, the lady's boyfriend came out of the bedroom into the living room. I looked at the lady and said I really didn't appreciate being lied to. The boyfriend told us they'd had a few people over for a few drinks and he told me who had been present. He said he and one of his guests had gotten into an argument and he had kicked him out. He said he shot his .308 caliber rifle into the air to make sure he left. It was apparent the boyfriend was highly intoxicated, so I told him he was under arrest for misconduct involving a weapon. His girlfriend got angry, stating he didn't do anything wrong, and she started cursing both Officer Lewis and me. I told her she too would be arrested if she interfered. This seemed to calm her down somewhat, and she quit cursing at us. I knew her boyfriend, the suspect, was on probation and I thought he was ordered in a court order not to consume alcohol, and now he was intoxicated and firing off a weapon.

I took both the .22 rifle and the 308 Winchester, to hold as evidence, and Officer Lewis transported the suspect to the police department, where a more in-depth interview was conducted. After being given his Miranda warning and signing a waiver, he told us another man, who was at his home at the time, tried to take the rifle away from him, and he pulled it through his hand, cutting the man's fingers on the rifle sight. He talked about the man he got in a verbal altercation with, as well as another man. He also named a 16-year-old girl who was at the residence at the time. Following the interview, the suspect was locked in a cell, and I had Officer Lewis stay at the police department, to guard the suspect, while I tried to locate the other parties who had been present at the residence.

I went back to the residence and again knocked on the door; when the girlfriend opened the door, I observed the 16-year-old girl, the suspect had named in the interview, to be sitting on the couch.

I told the girlfriend I needed to talk to the 16-year-old and I asked that she come outside the residence. It was evident the girl had been consuming alcohol by her mannerisms as well as the strong smell of alcohol on her breath. The girl told me she had witnessed the argument between the suspect and the man he'd kicked out of his home, and she said it scared her when the suspect grabbed the rifle and ran after the man when he'd gone outside. She said she was afraid he had shot him. She hadn't actually observed him shoot the rifle but had heard it. She also told me about the man who was injured when the rifle barrel was pulled through his hands when he was trying to take it from the suspect. When I asked her where she got the alcohol she had consumed, she said she'd consumed it while at the suspect's home. She said no one stopped her when she opened a can and started drinking it, so she had a couple more after that. I cited the teenager for minor consuming alcohol, then I took her to her residence and told her to tell her parents I would be by tomorrow to talk to them. She was told she would be contacted by the juvenile intake officer out of Kenai. I released her and told her it would probably be best if she stayed home the rest of the night, in that it was nearly 0300 hours. She said she wasn't going anywhere.

I responded to the residence of the man who was injured in the scuffle over the rifle. When I arrived at his residence, I observed lights were on, so I knocked on the door. The man came to the door, and I observed he had his right hand wrapped in a towel. Some blood was visible on the towel, and I asked if he needed medical assistance. He said he was just waiting until it stopped bleeding before he bandaged it. I told him why I was there, and he told me the same story I'd been told previously. He said when the suspect grabbed his .308 caliber Winchester, he had grabbed it by the barrel, trying to take it away from him, and the suspect had yanked it through his hand, cutting three of his fingers on the rifle sight. The man didn't appear to be intoxicated, although there was a mild odor of alcohol on his breath. He also named the same people when I asked him who all were at the party, with the exception of the 16-year-old girl. I asked why he didn't mention her, and he said he didn't want to get anyone in trouble, and he wasn't aware I knew. I thanked him for his time and made sure he didn't need any medical assistance, telling him I could call an EMT to bandage up his injury. He declined any medical assistance, and I left his residence.

I returned to the police department. After I got there, I wrote the suspect another citation for furnishing liquor to a minor, and served it to him inside the jail cell. I told him the 16-year-old had consumed beer that was at his home and I was going to hold him responsible for it. I then had the man sign a "Promise to Appear" form and then told Officer Lewis to take him home. I told him to refrain from consuming alcohol as directed by the court. Officer Lewis took the suspect home and then came back to the department.

I had started the paperwork on the case. I had labeled the two rifles and locked them in the evidence room. When he returned, I told Officer Lewis I would be contacting the suspect's probation officer first thing in the morning.

At approximately 0920 hours, I called the suspect's probation officer and relayed what had taken place. He directed me to arrest the suspect and transport him to Homer Jail. I called Officer Lewis and told him what had been ordered and that I would be back to town after delivering the suspect to Homer Jail. I told him to take calls until I returned.

I responded to the suspect's residence at approximately 1000 hours, and I had to wake him. I told him he was again under arrest and would have to come with me. I also told him his probation officer was not happy with him. I placed the suspect in handcuffs and transported him to the airport, where we were flown to Homer. A Homer police officer met the airplane, as was pre-arranged, and took custody of the suspect. I was able to take the next flight back to Seldovia. Now the paperwork really began.

After arriving back in Seldovia, I went to the 16-year old girl's residence and talked with her mother, explaining what had taken place and that they would have to talk to Eric Weatherby, the juvenile intake officer, when he came to Seldovia. The girl's mother told me her husband had gone to work but she would be letting him know when he got home. She said her daughter had told her most of the story before I had arrived. I bade the lady goodbye and left the residence for the Seldovia Police Department to work on the case file, readying it for the district attorney's office. (Case Closed by Arrest)

An Interesting Find

At approximately 1430 hours on February 16, 1985, I received a call requesting my presence at McDonald Spit. A man had been digging on his property to put a footing in for a shop building and he had found a couple bones. He thought the bones were of human origin but stated he was not sure. I told him he might want to quit digging until we knew more about what was going on. He assured me he had ceased all digging until he found out what the bones were.

I responded to McDonald Spit and contacted the man. He showed me where he was digging and he produced the two bones he had dug up. One appeared to be a human jaw bone and the other was a bone approximately 12" long, and could possibly be a human bone, as well. I asked the man what his plans were regarding the shop he was planning to build. I asked him if he could hold off until I could get the bones to the AST Laboratory to be identified. He said he only had a short time to build and hated the thought of waiting until the next year. He asked how long it would take the AST Lab to check the bones out. I told him I had no way of knowing and the lab was always very busy. I was concerned that he may be digging in an old burial ground, but until we had a definite identification on the bones, there was no way of knowing. I told him I wasn't ordering him to stop digging but he could end up digging up a lot of bones if he continued. He said he could possibly find another location for his shop and he told me he wouldn't continue to dig in that location. I thanked the man and took the bones with me to be readied for shipment to the AST Laboratory.

I packaged the two bones and sent them to the AST Lab with a description of the area where they were located. After approximately two months, I received a report from the lab. They found both the bones to be of human origin, stating most probably male, and of Eskimo descent, and approximately 35 years of age. The smaller bone was a jaw bone and the other, longer bone, was a left upper arm bone. The time of death was found to be most likely prehistoric.

The bones were returned to the police department, along with the report, and they were donated to the Seldovia Village Tribes Museum, to be put on display for the general public.

I called the man who found the bones and told him of the lab's report. I further told him that there was no way of knowing if the area was a burial ground or not but, if he found more bones, to let me know. That would possibly indicate a burial ground was located in that area. He said he'd decided on a new shop location and hadn't found any more bones when digging the footing in that area. (Case Closed by AST Lab Report)

ASSAULT AND CRIMINAL TRESPASS

On February 26, 1985, at approximately 1825 hours, two men showed up at the door of my residence, and each of them stated they wished to press charges against the other. The first man, who I'll refer to as suspect #1, said he had placed a second male, who I'll refer to as suspect #2, under citizen's arrest, charging him with criminal trespass for attempting to take an air compressor from suspect #1's property. Suspect #2 said he too wanted to make a citizen's arrest on suspect #1 for felony assault, stating suspect #1 had shot two tires out of his vehicle when he was trying to take the property of his that suspect #1 had failed to pay for.

I'd had people want to press charges against one another due to an altercation between them, but this was the first time I'd ever had two men want to make a citizen's arrest on each other at the same time. I should mention, the two men traveled 12 miles to my residence to make their citizen's arrests legal, and they were both traveling in the same vehicle. I'll bet that was an interesting trip.

Since we were at my residence, I told both men to meet me at the Seldovia Police Department where we'd deal with the matter. They were waiting when I arrived, and I told them I wanted to interview each of them separately and I wasn't going to tolerate any arguing or fighting. I told suspect #2 to wait outside. I decided to interview suspect #1 first.

I read suspect #1 his Miranda warning, and he signed the "Waiver of Rights" form. He told me suspect #2 arrived at his leased property and asked for payment for an air compressor suspect #1 had purchased from him. He went on to say he'd been short of funds and hadn't paid for the compressor in full, but he intended to pay for it when he got the funds to do so. He said he told suspect #2 he couldn't just walk onto his property and take anything and that he knew suspect #2 had to go before the court and get a court order. He told suspect #2 he would pay him but didn't have the money right now. He said suspect #2 stomped off and told him he was taking his air compressor. He indicated that he then went to his residence and got his rifle. He said the compressor was in a lower lot and he drove to that location. He said suspect #2 was trying to load the air compressor, with the assistance of a lady who had come with him, when he came out from town. He said he told suspect #2 to leave the compressor, and when he kept trying to load it, he shot both the right front tire and the right rear tire out on suspect #2's vehicle with his rifle, preventing him from leaving. He said, following a heated argument, he told suspect #2 that he was making a citizen's arrest and he would be delivering him to the Seldovia Police Department. A verbal argument followed, and then suspect #1 told him he could tell the officer about it when they got to town. He said he provided transportation for suspect #2 and for the lady who was with him. He went on to say that suspect #2 was intoxicated at the time of the argument.

I produced a "Citizen's Arrest Form," which suspect #1 filled out, charging suspect #2 with criminal trespass. I then excused suspect #1 and asked that he wait outside while I interviewed suspect #2.

I read the Miranda warning to him, and he also signed a "Waiver of Rights" form. He told me he had been visiting some friends in Seldovia and was telling them that suspect #1 owed him for a compressor. He said suspect #1 had gotten the compressor from him the previous year. He told them he was going out to pick it up and wondered if one or both of them would accompany him to be a witness that he didn't take anything but what was his. He said he knew suspect #1 and he'd probably say he took a number of items. The man he was visiting said he was tied up, but his wife probably could accompany him. He said they then traveled out to suspect #1's residence. He said he approached suspect #1 and told him he was there to pick up his compressor. The male told him to stay away from the compressor and that he would pay him when he got the money. He started to load the compressor anyway, when suspect #1 produced a rifle. He said suspect #1 told him to leave the compressor, and leave the property, and that he was pointing the rifle in his direction. He said the rifle didn't scare him and he told him he was taking the compressor. It was then that suspect #1 shot his right front and rear right tires out with the rifle. He said they had some words then, and suspect #1 told him he was under arrest, and that he was making a citizen's arrest. Suspect #1 told him he was going to bring him to the police in Seldovia. He said, to avoid a physical confrontation, he agreed to come with him, and he and the lady got into the subject's vehicle. When I ask him what kind of rifle suspect #1 had, he said it was a military-type rifle and that suspect #1 still had it in his vehicle. There was a strong smell of alcohol on suspect #2's breath, and I observed him to be a little unsteady on his feet. His eyes were bloodshot and his face was flushed. I asked him how much alcohol he had consumed and he said he'd only had a couple beers but, in my experience, I found him to be intoxicated. He said he wanted to make a citizen's arrest of suspect #1, as well. I provided a "Citizen's Arrest Form," and he filled it out, charging suspect #1 with a felony assault.

I called our local magistrate, Christine Kashevarof, and told her I had the two in custody, stemming from them both signing Citizen's Arrest Forms. I told her about the consumption of alcohol on suspect #2's part and that I felt he was intoxicated. The magistrate set some conditions of release that both of the subjects must agree to follow if they were to be released on their own recognizance.

I addressed both suspects. I told them the magistrate recognized the citizen's arrests as legal arrests and had told me they could be released on their own recognizance if they would have no further contact with each other, would obey all laws and ordinances, appear at any scheduled court appearances, and refrain from consuming alcohol. Suspect #1 said he'd agree to the stipulations, but suspect #2 said he was going to have a beer when all of this was over, regardless of what anyone said.

Suspect #1 signed the "Promise to Appear" form and was released after he relinquished his Remington .223 caliber rifle to the police, to be kept as evidence until this matter was over.

Suspect #2 was told to empty his pockets and he was fingerprinted; mug shots were taken and he was booked into the Seldovia jail facility. He was still defiant, stating that no one could tell him he couldn't drink. I told him he wouldn't be drinking anything tonight. He was not happy, but by the next morning he told me he had changed his mind, and he signed the "Promise to Appear" form. He agreed to the stipulations, including the one which ordered him not to consume alcohol.

Within two months, the district attorney had dismissed both cases, not wanting to waste the court's time on the two frivolous complaints. The rifle was returned to suspect #1, and the case was closed.

Sometimes the police get involved in cases they feel will most probably not ever see a courtroom. These cases still take the same amount of time, if not more, to investigate and put in writing for the district attorney. Sometimes an officer has to hold his tongue and not express his personal feelings, even though he so desperately wants to. This was one of those cases. A lot of time and paperwork, but no real conclusion. Oh well, I'm getting paid so I'll continue to bite my tongue and not voice my opinion when it does no good or change the outcome of a case. (Case Closed by Citizen's Arrests)

Burglary of a Local Grocery Store

O
n April 19, 1985, at approximately 2045 hours, the Seldovia Police Department was called regarding a burglary at a local grocery store. The caller said it appeared the burglar(s) exited through an upper window in the store, as it was open, and foot tracks were visible. I called Officer Lewis on the radio and asked that he meet me at the store.

Officer Lewis and I arrived at the store and were met by the store owners. We were told they had found a window ajar in the upper level of the store and they thought the burglar(s) had left through that window. They said numerous items had been taken, which they thought would run into hundreds of dollars once they figured out what all was missing.

In checking the area where the window was found to be ajar, the officer found a footprint in some sawdust below the window that was unique, in that it had two circles on the heel portion, which overlapped one another. Further footprint evidence was located outside the window area, on the metal roof. The footprint matched the print inside the building below the window, also having the two interlocking circles on the heel. No other evidence of a forced entry was found, and the tracks we had found only led away from the store. This indicated the burglar had left by the window but no evidence pointed to him gaining entry at that location. It appeared that the window had been opened from the inside. We agreed and felt that at least one burglar had exited through the window. We also felt the burglar was someone who was fairly agile, since they would have had to jump off the roof to the ground if they did exit through the window. Prior to leaving the store, we requested the store owners get a list of items taken, as close as possible, so we could come to a monetary figure. This would determine what degree felony would be charged if, or when, the burglar(s) were ever caught.

Officer Lewis and I went to the police department and developed a list of suspects who were in the area at the time, and someone who we thought would, and could, burglarize the store. We came up with a list of six people who were in town and who we thought would be capable of pulling this off.

On April 22, at approximately 2230 hours, I saw one of the people Officer Lewis and I had listed as a possible suspect in the burglary of the store. He was coming out of the other store in town, and I stopped him. I asked that he let me see the bottom of the tennis shoes he was wearing. He asked why, and I told him I just wanted to see the tread, in that I was going to buy some shoes, and I sure liked the look of his, but I wanted a pair that had a good tread. He showed me the tread on the tennis shoes, and I observed two circles that overlapped one another. I felt strongly that he was the one who had left the footprint near the window of the other store, but I'd been fooled in the past by jumping to conclusions in an investigation. I told him, as a matter of fact, that I knew he'd burglarized the other store. I told him I was in the middle of another problem that I had to deal with, so we couldn't talk right now. I did assure him we would be talking. I told him he would be a lot better off if he was to man up and do the right thing, and get out in front of this. I said he should come to us before we came to him, and then I left. Four days later, the suspect contacted Officer Lewis at approximately 2230 hours and told him he had committed the burglary of the store. He took the officer to a location behind a building, where he had stashed most of the items he'd taken. Officer Lewis called me on the radio, requesting I come to the police department, stating he had someone who wanted to talk to me about the burglary of the store. I believe my talk with the suspect a few days earlier had concerned him greatly, and he thought, by coming forward it would go easier on him. Maybe it was his conscience he couldn't deal with. Either way, we had our burglar.

I responded to the police department and found the suspect and Officer Lewis to be waiting. Officer Lewis told me what he had been told and he showed me the items he'd recovered behind a building.

I interviewed the suspect after reading him his Miranda warning, and after he'd signed a "Waiver of Rights" form. Because he was a juvenile, I asked him if he wanted his parent/guardian present during the interview, and he said he did not. He said he'd hid in the upstairs portion of the store until after the owner had locked up and gone home. He said he then came out of hiding and started filling shopping bags with items from the store. He said he set the items outside the back door of the store and then locked the back door, prior to leaving. He said he then exited the building through the window on the second floor, he then crossed the roof, and jumped off the roof. I asked if he had opened the window and then exited and then reached back inside and cranked the window shut as far as he could. He said he had closed it as far as he could. He said he then carried the items and stashed them behind the building next door to the store. He said he took what he could carry and went over to a friend's house. The two of them then ate some Pop-Tarts and some granola bars. He further said he had told his friend about the burglary and that he had shared the items with him.

I told the suspect he was free to go, following the interview, and that I would be submitting the case to the juvenile intake officer, Eric Weatherby, and he and his parent, or guardian, would have to meet with him when he came to town.

I then filled out an application for a search warrant for the second suspect's residence. I listed all the items off the list I'd gotten from the store owners on the application. The magistrate granted the search warrant, and Officer Lewis and I responded to the suspect's residence. When we arrived, the suspect was home. I told him why we were there and I presented him with a copy of the warrant. The search did result in a number of items that were listed on the warrant as items taken in the store burglary. He admitted the items we'd found came from the burglary but stated he didn't know they were stolen until after they had been eating them. Officer Lewis located a sea otter pelt in the back room of the residence and it was taken as evidence of another crime. We were aware no natives lived at the residence; one has to be a Native American to own, or even possess, a sea otter hide.

Following the search of the suspect's residence, he was asked to accompany us to the police department, where he could be further interviewed. He agreed to come voluntarily, and we left his residence and responded to the police department, where, following being given his Miranda warning, and after signing his "Waiver of Rights" form, the suspect was interviewed. Because he was a juvenile, he was asked if he wanted his guardian present and he stated he did not. He stated he had received some of the stolen items but, when he had participated in eating them, he did not know they were stolen. He said he found out afterward and that he hadn't consumed any since. When I inquired about the sea otter pelt, the suspect said he didn't know anything about it and that it had been at the residence for a number of years. I released him and asked if he wanted a ride back to his residence; he declined the offer. I told him that he and his parent/guardian would have to meet with Eric Weatherby, the juvenile intake officer, when he came to town on charges of receiving stolen property. He told me he'd tell his mother.

The case was forwarded to the Kenai Juvenile Intake Office, and Eric Weatherby did come to Seldovia to meet with the suspects and their parents or guardians. I do not know what the end result was. (Case Closed by Investigation and Referral to Juvenile Intake)

Policing a Small Bush Community: My Philosophy

I 've been asked on a number of different occasions what my secret was to being able to hold a police officer's position for nearly thirty-two years in a small bush community. In most small communities, I'm told, an officer usually only serves two to five years. I've also been told the politics get so fierce that they move on, not wanting to deal with them over and over again. I certainly can relate to the politics being such that an employee would want to change employment, but I hung on for a couple very important reasons. I wanted to be home with my family and, secondly, I had a job that was supplying a wage where I could make this happen without having to leave home to find employment.

I had no formal police training when I started, prior to going through the Police Academy. I learned by doing the job and by relying on others who knew the job for advice. I credit my longevity to all the advice I got from the officers of the Alaska State Troopers and the dispatchers and officers of the Homer Police Department.

I don't have any big secrets when it comes to how to effectively police a small community. I do have a philosophy that I'll share with you though. In my view, it's very simple and based on common sense. I had parents who raised me, above everything, to be honest, and to give an employer eight hours work for eight hours pay. I was taught to show respect to everyone, whether you actually respected them or not. The day I was hired, I took an oath to treat everyone equally and fairly, and I took that oath seriously. I took it so seriously, in fact, that I even pledged to myself that, as long as I was in office, I would, "*Treat a drunk like a preacher and I'd treat a preacher like a drunk.*" In other words, I would treat everyone equally, regardless of who I was dealing with. I tried hard to uphold that oath, and I feel I accomplished that goal throughout my career.

I stayed for all those years, through all the petty politics and some backstabbing, for, as aforementioned, a couple reasons. I wanted to be more involved in the raising of my daughter and I wanted to be a husband to my wife. I missed so much by having to work away from home for all those years, but finally, I now had a job where I could stay home, and I really didn't want to be forced to leave again to find other employment. I really enjoyed being home. Because of these two reasons, I put up with a lot of political backstabbing, rumors that ran rampant at times, and a lower wage than other officers in other departments were being paid. I also love Seldovia, and I think you have to love the town you serve in. I made some sacrifices so I would be able to share in the upbringing of my daughter from the age of ten, and I wanted to actually be able to stay home with my wife. This was the most important thing to me, and it was well worth any sacrifices I had to make on the job.

So now my secret, which is really no secret at all, is out. I can only say a man has to be happy at home, he has to be willing to work the job he's been hired for, and he must love where he resides. You must do it honestly and treat people with dignity and respect. I think, if there is a secret to staying employed as a police officer in a small community for a long period of time, that would be it

1985: ANOTHER BUSY YEAR

I probably sound a little like a scratched record, but I want to give you a feel for the number and type of calls that come into a small-town police department. In 1985, we investigated two vehicle accidents with one who left the scene and was later charged, we investigated one case of custodial interference as an agency assist for a police department out of Oregon, we investigated four assaults, two deaths, one sexual assault of a minor, charged one person with misconduct with weapons, we had seven DWIs, we impounded one vehicle, we investigated four burglaries, one of a business and three in residences, charged one juvenile with minor consuming alcohol, wrote a citation for negligent driving, one residence was vandalized, one case of criminal mischief was investigated, we diverted one suicide attempt, and responded to one domestic violence call. All of this, with the daily bar checks, traffic control, the animal control issues, and the citizens' assists, kept us quite busy during 1985.

It may sound like, over a year's time, this wasn't all that many cases, but there were only two of us covering the calls seven days a week, 24 hours a day. When I talk about case investigations, each case is different, and each case takes time to investigate. Some can be brought to a conclusion quickly and some can take days or months to close. In many cases, we have to depend on other agencies for assistance, and they too have a priority they have to address, and that slows down the investigation for us, as well. I'm in no way complaining, only trying to explain the responsibilities of the job. We didn't ever have any problem finding something to do.

THEFT OF A VEHICLE

On August 6, 1985, at approximately 1000 hours, I received a call from a local resident reporting the theft of a vehicle from the airport and it had been located in a ditch in the East Addition. She stated the owner lived in Anchorage and had a summer home here in Seldovia. She had called him prior to reporting the vehicle stolen, and he told her he had not given permission to anyone to use his vehicle. The complainant further told me that she had heard two of our local teenagers had taken the vehicle, but she did not want to divulge her source. She said they wanted to remain confidential, however, she did tell me the two teenagers' names.

I contacted one teenager, who I felt would be more forthcoming than the other, and I interviewed him in the presence of his mother. He readily admitted to being involved in the taking of the vehicle, but said they were walking in the parking lot of the airport when the other teenager jumped into the vehicle and started it up. He said, "He told me to jump in, so I did." He told me they drove around town, and to the Outside Beach, and then he drove it back into town. He said he wanted to take it back to the airport, but his friend told him to take him home first. When he took his friend home, he said he was trying to turn around when he backed off the road and into a ditch. He told me they tried to get the vehicle out but they couldn't, so they left it there, and he walked home. I told the teenager and his mother that they would have to see the juvenile intake officer when he came to town, and the boy's mother said they would be there, just to let them know when.

Following that interview, I called the residence of the other teenager involved in the theft, and he and his step-father came to the police department, where I interviewed him in the presence of his step-father. The teenager told me the other teenager entered the vehicle at the airport and started it. He said he was then told to jump in, and they drove all around Seldovia and to the Outside Beach. He did admit to also driving the vehicle, but said his friend was the one who got the vehicle stuck. He said it was his friend's idea. As I did with his friend, I told him and his step-father that they would have to see the juvenile intake officer when he came to town, and I told them I would be letting them know when he was coming.

A local mechanic was hired to remove the vehicle from the ditch and to check for any damages it may have sustained in the incident.

I told both the teenagers, and their parents, I would be sending the report to the juvenile intake officer, Eric Weatherby, and they would have to meet with him when he came to town. I told them they would be responsible for any damage to the vehicle and any gas they used would have to be replaced.

As in many of the juvenile cases, I did not find out the disposition of the case, but I do know the teenagers and their parents did meet with Eric Weatherby when he came to town. I'm sure restitution was ordered and, as in most of the juvenile cases, the two were most probably placed on informal probation for a six-month or one-year period. This was customary for teenagers who didn't have a criminal past and were first-time offenders. (Case Closed by Referral to Juvenile Intake)

SKIFF STOLEN AND TAKEN OUT OF SELDOVIA

On September 23, 1985, at approximately 1215 hours, a man came to the Seldovia police department and reported that he had gone to the boat harbor to check his skiff, and it was gone. He said he checked all over the harbor but could not find his boat. He had used the skiff the day before, he said. He described the boat as a white, 14-foot fiberglass seine skiff with a 40 horsepower outboard. He said the skiff had a well in it for the motor. He told me he hadn't given anyone permission to use the skiff.

At approximately 1310 hours, on the same day, I took the owner around Seldovia Bay in the public safety boat in search of his skiff. We searched the entire bay, but did not find the skiff.

After returning to the boat harbor, I asked the harbor master if anyone from any of the local villages had been in town, and if they had come by skiff. I was told two men from English Bay, now called Nanwelak, had been in town the day before, but he didn't know how they went home. They had flown in, but he didn't know if they were still in town. He gave me their names, and I went to my office and called both airlines who service this area, and asked if either of the suspects had flown home with them. I was told by Homer Air personnel that the two had flown into Seldovia the previous morning but hadn't flown back with them. After calling Cook Inlet Aviation, and getting a negative reply to the two flying back with them, I called English

Bay and talked with a friend I knew in the village, and asked him to check and see if the skiff was there. I gave him a description of it. I also asked that he check to see if the suspects were back in the village. After approximately an hour, I received a call back from my friend, and he said the two suspects were back in the village, but he couldn't locate the skiff I'd described to him. I knew both of the suspects, and I asked that he have the one I knew best call me, and I gave him the police number.

Approximately half an hour later, I received a call from the suspect. I told him I had information that he had taken a skiff from the Seldovia Harbor and I wanted the skiff back. He admitted to taking the skiff, and told me he and his friend, the second suspect, were partying aboard the *Jo Ann Marie* and had taken the skiff to English Bay, but he said he didn't know where it was now. They were intoxicated when they took it, he said, and they failed to tie it up when they landed on the beach below the village. He told me he was going to bring it back but he could not find it. He said he finally did see it floating about halfway between the village and Point Phigibshi. He said he had no way of going to get it. I told him not to leave the village and that I would be in touch with him.

At approximately 1635 hours, I took the victim on the public safety boat, and we traveled south to Dangerous Cape in an effort to locate his skiff. We did find the skiff grounded on some rocks inside Dangerous Cape. A small surf was running on the beach, so I could only drop the victim off on the beach and back off so the public safety boat didn't get beat up on the rocks or on the beach. The owner took a long line with him when he went to check the skiff, to secure it so it wouldn't float away when the tide did float it again. When he came back to the boat, he told me the two oars, which were tied inside the boat, and the oarlocks were missing. He said the lower unit on the outboard was busted and the propeller was ruined. The steering stock was also damaged, he said. He said he only had one gas tank in the skiff when he had it, and now there were two tanks, so they must have stolen another tank before they left the Seldovia Boat Harbor. He said it was secured now, and he'd come back to get it at high tide. He would have to take the skiff out of the water and turn it over, he said, before he could ascertain if the bottom of the boat had been damaged. I told him I'd be pursuing the case further, and we went back to Seldovia. Prior to going back to Seldovia, I took a series of 35 mm pictures of the area and the boat.

While we went to locate the boat, Officer Jerry Lewis interviewed the second suspect telephonically. The man told him he'd thought his buddy had permission to use the skiff. He claimed he didn't know it was stolen. He said they were partying aboard the *Dee Dee II* and were both intoxicated when they left the harbor. He said they left Seldovia around 0500 hours on September 9. He said he had no idea the skiff had floated off the beach in English Bay either.

The victim, with the assistance of another Seldovia resident, traveled to the Dangerous Cape area and retrieved the skiff at high tide. The skiff was towed back to Seldovia, where it was taken out of the water and inspected thoroughly. Along with the aforementioned damage, the bottom of the boat was chipped in numerous places where the sides meet the bottom. The boat would have to have a lot of fiberglass work done before it could be used for seining. I took a number of 35 mm photographs of all the damage to the boat.

On September 29, I flew to English Bay, where I conducted another interview with suspect #2 in the Tribal Council Office. He told me suspect #1 had told him he had gotten permission from the owner of the skiff when they were in the Linwood Bar earlier in the day. He also said both gas tanks were already in the skiff when he and suspect #1 got in it to go to English Bay. He said his buddy was the person responsible, and he would not have gone with him had he known it was stolen. He said he didn't find out it was stolen until they were in English Bay.

Upon returning to Seldovia from English Bay, a local teacher came to the police department to report that a gas tank had been stolen from his Zodiac, which was moored in the boat harbor. Upon showing him the extra tank that was found in the stolen skiff, he positively identified it and he was given his property.

The case was sent to the district attorney and a summons complaint was served on suspect #1 charging him with criminal mischief in the 4th degree after a plea bargain was reached between the district attorney and the suspect's court-appointed public defender. The felony charges were never charged, much to the dismay of the Seldovia Police Department. The second suspect was not charged due to a lack of evidence, even though the officers of the Seldovia Police Department strongly felt he was knowingly involved in the theft of the skiff and the extra gas tank.

The first suspect pled guilty to the lesser charge and was sentenced to forty-five days in jail with twenty-five suspended; he was ordered to pay $2,242.30 in restitution to the owner of the skiff and was ordered to undergo alcohol counseling at SKIAP (South Peninsula Inc. Alcoholism Program), which was located in Seldovia. He was also placed on probation for a period of two years. As stated, suspect #2 was never charged in the case.

Both Officer Lewis and I felt strongly that felony charges should have been brought in this case. Had it not been for us finding the skiff the same day it was reported stolen, the tide likely would have taken it out to sea, or it could have been destroyed on the rocks where it went ashore. It would have only taken a moderate southwest wind to create a swell on the beach that would have beaten the boat to pieces. Just another case the district attorney didn't want to fully prosecute, in my opinion. I hope the suspect learned his lesson through the sentence that was handed down, but it certainly was not near what he should have received. (Case Closed by Summons Complaint)

DEATH BY DROWNING

On October 26, 1985, at approximately 0055, I was awakened by a phone call from the US Coast Guard. They reported they had taken a call from a distraught female who told them she needed help, that her boyfriend had fallen into the water in the Seldovia Boat Harbor, and she couldn't get him out. She asked that they call the police department for assistance.

Officer Lewis was out of town, and I was the only officer working. I called the harbormaster and told him of the report, then I responded to the boat harbor. When I arrived, I found the distraught lady to be on "F" float, and she was yelling and waving her arms. She pointed in the direction of the airplane float, and I ran past her to that location. Floating face down was her boyfriend, a local man who I knew very well. I could not reach him, so I grabbed an oar out of a skiff, near the airplane float, and I pulled his lifeless body in where I could grab him. I pulled him up on the float and turned him onto his back. It was then the harbormaster arrived. I checked for a pulse and was unable to find one. We started CPR, with me doing compressions, while the harbormaster did the breaths. There was a lot of foam in the mouth of the victim, and the harbormaster kept wiping it away, and kept giving him breaths when I'd stop the compressions. We continued our effort for what seemed like forever, until the EMTs finally arrived. There were five EMTs and they took over the CPR.

The girlfriend, who had called the Coast Guard, was hysterical, and one of the EMTs was comforting her. She was found to be highly intoxicated and was very hard to interview, but I questioned her as to what had taken place. She said she and her boyfriend had been coming down to the boat, where they were staying, and he had stumbled and fallen overboard. He was holding onto the bull rail of the float when she had run to call the Coast Guard. She was devastated and wondered why he hadn't hung on until she could get help.

Doctor Reynolds showed up on the scene, and the victim was transported on a stretcher to the waiting ambulance. The EMTs continued CPR while moving him. The victim was loaded into the ambulance, and the doctor and the EMTs continued CPR for nearly an hour before finally giving up on their efforts. I was told they had him back for a little while, but then lost him again.

Our EMT crew was one of the best in the state, and, with the doctor's assistance, I'm sure if anyone could have saved him, it would have been them.

The victim's drowning had a huge impact on Seldovia and its residents. He was a very well-liked man and had been around Seldovia for a number of years. He played banjo and would often entertain his friends. He'll always be in the memories of all who knew him. Rest in peace, my friend. (Case Closed)

A ROLLING ROAD BLOCK

O n December 28, 1985, at approximately 0015 hours, Officer Lewis was on patrol when he observed a pickup driving down Main Street, which had signaled to turn right, then made an abrupt left turn into the parking lot of the store. Due to the time of the morning, and the erratic behavior of the driver, Officer Lewis decided he would check to see if everything was okay. He parked beside the vehicle, exited, and walked over to the pickup. He observed a female to be the only person in the vehicle, and she was sitting with her head down, as if she were asleep. The officer asked if she had a problem, and she was startled by his presence. She told the officer she was doing fine and when she did, the officer observed her speech to be very slurred and, upon closer observation, he smelled a strong odor of alcohol coming from the cab of the vehicle. The pickup was still running, and Officer Lewis directed her to turn the ignition off. She failed to do as directed, and he opened the door to shut the vehicle off himself. When the officer reached into the vehicle, the lady put the pickup in reverse and started backing toward Main Street.

Officer Lewis, in an effort to keep from being hit by the door, grabbed the door and held on, and he was dragged out onto Main Street. She stopped the vehicle to put it into low, and the officer let go, rolling onto the pavement away from the truck. The lady then sped away in an easterly direction down Main Street. Officer Lewis ran to his patrol vehicle and took off in pursuit. He called me as soon as he entered his vehicle and told me he was in pursuit, and that the driver was DWI and had turned on Seldovia Street off Main Street, heading in a northerly direction. He was requesting assistance.

The four-way intersection, located at Alder and Seldovia Streets, was visible to me from my residence and from the living room, I observed the pickup, with Officer Lewis right behind her with his overhead lights on, go through the stop sign and continue in a northerly direction. I grabbed my police gear, ran to my patrol vehicle, and took off, hurrying to catch up. I had my overhead lights on, but due to the time of the night, I avoided using the siren, not wanting to wake up people in town. I caught up with Officer Lewis and the pickup approximately 1¼ miles out of town. Both Officer Lewis and the pickup were driving in the middle of the roadway, and I told the officer I was going to try and pass the lady to get in front, where we could possibly slow her down. We were on a straight stretch of road, and Officer Lewis pulled to the right, allowing me to pass him. After getting around Officer Lewis, I turned on my siren and, to my surprise, the lady pulled to the right side of the road and allowed me to pass. We were now approximately 2 miles out of Seldovia, and I told Officer Lewis on the radio that I was going to try and do a running road block.

NOTE: A running road block is when the following officer gets up close to the back of the fleeing vehicle, and the lead officer starts applying his brakes, and stays in the middle of the roadway, thus making it impossible for the suspect to pass.

As I started slowing down, Officer Lewis moved up close to her rear bumper. We gradually brought the maneuver into play and were successful in getting the lady to stop. As soon as she stopped, I exited my vehicle and ran back to her pickup, where I jerked the door open and grabbed for the keys. Luckily, I was able to shut the ignition off because the lady had thrown the manual drive vehicle in low gear and was letting off the clutch when I was able to get it stopped. After the vehicle was stopped, I directed the driver to exit the vehicle, and she just looked at me. I reached in, grabbed her left arm, and began pulling her from the pickup. She made a roundhouse right swing and hit me right in the nose with her fist, breaking my glasses, which I wore at the time. I was not expecting that. I jerked her out of the pickup and put her face down on the roadway. I was really mad, as well as hurting, so I told Officer Lewis he should handcuff her so I didn't get too rough with her. He smiled at me and said, "A tough one, huh?"

Officer Lewis put the lady in his vehicle and I drove the pickup into a pull off near where we had stopped. We then proceeded to the police department. When we arrived at the police department, the lady had passed out, and we had a very difficult time waking her. When she did come to, she cursed us and was screaming at the top of her voice. I'm sure anyone within earshot would have thought we were practicing some of that police brutality. We did get her inside and, after getting inside, and her feeling the heat, she again passed out. She was too intoxicated to even put her through field sobriety tests or to make any rational decisions regarding her right to an independent test, to blow the breathalyzer, or to sign a number of other papers, relating to a DWI arrest. No interview could be conducted, so the voice recordings and the police report would have to suffice.

I made the decision to call the EMTs and have the lady checked out, because I didn't want to take the chance of her aspirating into her lungs and dying in the jail cell. The EMTs came down and checked her, but couldn't give me any recommendations because they didn't really know if she would have a problem or not. Dr. Larry Reynolds was called and he came to the police department. After he'd examined the lady, he recommended we put a guard with her in the jail cell to ensure she didn't have a problem. He advised that we keep her on her stomach so she wouldn't aspirate into her lungs if she did have a problem.

Dr. Reynold's suggestions were taken, and a female guard was called in, and spent the better part of the night with the lady in the cell. She was given a handheld radio and told to call if any problem arose. Luckily, no problems did occur, and the lady slept the night and most of the morning away.

After the lady did wake up, and was halfway sober, I brought her out of the cell and explained to her what had taken place, after she told me she didn't remember anything that had gone on. She was somewhat embarrassed by what had happened and she apologized to me. I told her she was arrested and would be charged with DWI and failure to stop at the direction of a police officer. I mentioned that she had assaulted me but I told her, due to her state of intoxication, I would overlook that charge. I told her she would have to come up with $1000 cash if she wanted to bail out. The Court had set a bail of $500 for each A class misdemeanor charged. She asked if she could make a phone call and she called a family member. He came to the police department and bailed her out. Along with the $1000 fine, she had to promise to appear for all scheduled court hearings, she had to obey all laws and ordinances, and she had to agree to refrain from consuming alcoholic beverages until this case was over. She also had to agree not to leave the Third Judicial District without first obtaining permission from the court. After she signed her Conditions of Release form, she was released from custody.

On her court date the lady pled guilty to both DWI and failure to stop at the direction of a police officer. On the DWI charge, she was sentenced to thirty days in jail with all but 72 hours suspended, and she was told she could spend the three days in the Seldovia Jail. She was fined $500 with $250 suspended, and her operator license was suspended for ninety days, and she was given a seven-day license. She was further ordered to have no criminal violation for a period of one year. She was also ordered to undertake alcohol screening at SKIAP. On the charge of failure to stop at the direction of a police officer, she was fined $250 and verbally reprimanded for her actions on the day in question.

In a small town like Seldovia, one would think nothing like this would ever take place, but in my career, I had a few people who chose not to pull over when I activated my emergency gear. The small size of a community really doesn't mean the people are that different from people in larger communities. The perception is that very little activity takes place in a smaller area. I guess I thought the same thing before I put on the badge and found out for myself. In larger cities, they just have more people to deal with the problems and, due to there being more people, there are more problems, I guess. The advantage here is that they really can't run too far. (Case Closed by Arrest)

THEFT OF A THREE-WHEELER

On May 2, 1986, at approximately 1720 hours, a man came to the Seldovia Police Department and reported that a three-wheeler, which was parked in the Jakolof Bay area, had the tires and other parts taken off it. The complainant stated he was looking out for a friend's property while he and his wife were away and, in checking the property, he'd found their three-wheeler had been stripped. He said the owners kept the machine near their residence, under a tarp, and he had noticed the front fender uncovered, with the machine's headlight sitting on it. Closer examination revealed the tires had been taken and the controls were also missing. He said he had checked the property a few days earlier, and the three-wheeler was still intact. It had been stripped in the last couple days, he said.

Officer Lewis responded to the Jakolof Bay residence and observed the three-wheeler in question to have its wheels and rear hubs missing, as well as its controls. The headlight had been taken out and was lying on the fender of the machine. After taking a series of photographs, and making a cast of a footprint beside the machine, the officer returned to town.

David Bishop, a part-time officer, who was helping us out at the time, said he had helped a local teenager take some tires off of rims and put them on rims that were on the teenager's machine. He also had hubs he was going to change out, as well as some controls he told him about.

On May 5, at approximately 1600 hours, I stopped the suspect Officer Bishop had told us about, when I observed him driving his

185

three-wheeler downtown. I asked where he'd gotten the tires he had on his machine. He said another teenager, whom he named, had given them to him. I thanked him and I let him continue on his way. I had discovered over the past few years that sometimes it's good to just plant a seed if you already have a good idea of what will grow from it. I knew the parts off the three-wheeler, which were stolen, were not going out of town, so I thought I'd give the teenager something to think about. I always felt a little worry never hurt anyone; in fact, in some instances, it helped out considerably.

At approximately 1800 hours, the same day I had stopped him, the suspect was reported to have been observed going out of the Jakolof Bay Road, possibly going back to the scene of the crime. We waited a couple hours, then Officer Lewis and I went to the residence of the young man and questioned him in front of his mother. On this occasion, the suspect admitted to taking the tires and the controls off the machine. He said he'd heard some seventh graders talking about a three-wheeler that was parked out at Jakolof Bay. He named another teenager who took the headlight, and an older teenager who said he was going to get the taillight off the machine. When told the headlight wasn't taken, that it was just removed from the machine, he told us the headlight that was on the fender of the three-wheeler was the one out of the other teenager's machine that didn't work. I told him I wanted everything he had taken off the three-wheeler, and he went into a shed on the property and brought me the controls, and the hubs to the machine.

I asked him why he was going out to Jakolof Bay a couple hours ago, and he said he had gotten frightened when I'd talked to him about the tires. He said he was going out to put them back on the machine. He said he'd put the tires back on their own rims, and then had taken them, and had put them back on the machine.

I informed him and his mother that I would be sending the case to the juvenile intake officer in Kenai, and she and her son would have to meet with him when he came to town. I told them I would advise them when I found out when he would be coming to town.

Officer Lewis and I then went to the other teenager's home, who had reportedly taken the headlight. We talked to him in the presence of his mother, and he admitted to taking the headlight and told us that he was told it was okay to take it, that it was abandoned. I told him the machine was under a tarp, on the property of the victims, and he was telling us he thought it was abandoned. I told him he would be charged with the theft, and he and his parent would have to meet with Eric Weatherby of the Kenai Peninsula Juvenile Intake System. I told him I'd think up a better story before he met with Mr. Weatherby. I suggested the truth might be what he wanted to tell him. Following my suggestion, the teenager told me he stole the headlight and he said he was sorry. He took the headlight out of his machine, while we were there, and gave it to me. I thanked him and told him being honest is the best policy and, I'm sure, if he needed a headlight so bad, he could find another way to get it. Maybe even do some work, and earn the money to buy a new one. With that, Officer Lewis and I left the residence.

Mr. Weatherby did come to Seldovia and he met with the two teenagers and their parents. He told me he had placed both boys on informal probation and gave them a curfew of 2200 hours and, if they failed to obey the directives, he told them he would think about putting them in McLoughlin Youth Center for a while. He said maybe they would fear McLoughlin enough that they would stay out of trouble. I delivered Mr. Weatherby to the airport and thanked him for his help. (Case Closed by Referral to Juvenile Intake)

Assisting the Alaska State Troopers

On June 26, 1986, at approximately 1015 hours, Cpl. Dan Weatherly of the Alaska State Troopers called and asked if I could assist them in an arrest in English Bay, now called Nanwalek. He said, due to him being the only trooper on duty, he had to go to one of the Russian villages on a domestic violence call. He was told a man in the village was intoxicated and had reportedly assaulted his mother. He said, even though the man had been kicked out of her home, he kept coming back and repeatedly attempted to get back inside. The VPSO, out of Port Graham, was going to go but felt he needed assistance because the suspect had been violent with him in the past. I told Cpl. Weatherly I would call an airplane and head that way. He asked that I house the suspect in the Seldovia jail and arraign him in Seldovia before Magistrate Christine Kashevarof in the Seldovia court.

I flew to Port Graham and met with the VPSO. We then flew to English Bay and asked the pilot to wait for us. The VPSO and I met with the mother of the suspect and the complainant, the victim's husband. Both told the same story. They said the suspect had come to visit and was intoxicated when he arrived. He assaulted his mother by kicking her in the leg and in the stomach. He and the complainant got into a fight. The suspect was kicked out, and told not to come back. The complainant said the suspect returned numerous times and attempted to get into the residence and, on each occasion, the complainant kept him from entering.

After leaving the victim's and the complainants' residence, we found the suspect on the back road, where he was again headed for his mother's and stepfather's residence. He was taken into custody without incident, and we walked him to the airport where we boarded the waiting airplane. Larry Thompson, owner or operator of Homer Air Service, took the VPSO back to Port Graham and dropped him off, and then delivered the suspect and me to Seldovia. I transported the suspect to the police department, where he was booked in and interviewed.

After reading the suspect his Miranda rights warning and, after he signed his Waiver of Rights form, I interviewed him. The suspect admitted to being at his mother's home and he admitted to getting into a fight with his stepfather, the complainant. He also told me his stepfather had kicked him out of the residence and he did try to get back into the home, but he adamantly denied assaulting his mother. When further questioned, he admitted to trying to get back into the residence on several occasions. The suspect was then incarcerated in the Seldovia Jail, awaiting his arraignment. I called for a jail guard to guard the suspect until he could be arraigned. Due to his intoxicated state, the officer asked that the arraignment be put off until the next day. Another guard was hired to cover the rest of the suspect's stay.

I filled out three formal complaints, charging the suspect with disorderly conduct, assault in the 4th degree, and attempted criminal trespass. On June 28, at approximately 1100 hours, the suspect was arraigned before Magistrate Kashevarof; the suspect pled not guilty to the charges. The magistrate set a trial date, and set bail at $500, and ordered him not to consume alcoholic beverages, not to contact the complainant or the victim directly or indirectly, to not leave the Third Judicial District without written permission of the court, and to obey all laws and ordinances. When the suspect couldn't make bail, I called Homer Airlines and made arrangements to take the suspect to Homer Jail. The Seldovia Jail, at this time, was only a holding facility and couldn't be utilized to hold prisoners for trial or for letting court-ordered sentences to be served. The airplane arrived, and I delivered the suspect to the Homer Jail.

I never received a disposition from the court on this case, so I don't know the outcome, but I was not called to testify, so I'm assuming the suspect pled guilty or no-contest at the pre-trial hearing and he was sentenced.

Since we had a contract with the Department of Public Safety, I often assisted the troopers in investigations and arrests in the villages. It seemed to always be alcohol/drug-related cases, and there seemed to always be some violence involved. The VPSOs often called for assistance as well, and I would respond if the weather would let us fly. I became well acquainted with people from both Port Graham and English Bay/ Nanwalek, and there are many wonderful, upstanding people in both villages. It's too bad we seem only to hear about the ones who cause all the problems. (Case Closed by Arrest)

CHILD NEGLECT

On August 15, 1986, at 2130 hours, when doing a bar check at the Linwood Bar, I observed the 11-year-old daughter of a local lady enter the bar and ask if anyone had seen her mother. Another lady in the bar told the girl that her mother had purchased some liquor and had then gone up Seldovia Bay to party with a couple of her friends. The 11-year-old left the bar, and I called Officer John Gruber, who was assisting me at the time, and directed him to go do a welfare check on the other children at the residence of the lady who had gone up the bay. Officer Gruber responded to the residence and, after doing a welfare check, reported the three boys, ages four, six and eight were all out front of the residence when he arrived, and they told him they had not eaten. The house was without heat and was very dirty, with items were thrown everywhere, and the home had a very pungent odor.

I immediately called the Division of Family and Youth Services (DFYS) and, because it was a weekend, I left a message. Within an hour, the DFYS Officer called me back. I described the case to him, and he told me to take the children out of the home and take them to a safe home. He said, if the mother showed up and was sober, the officer could tell her where her children were, but if she was still intoxicated, to keep the children in a safe home. I called a local man who had stated he and his wife would like to be a safe home if it were ever needed. He readily agreed to take the children in and care for them until he heard from me again.

I reported to Officer Gruber what the DFYS Officer had told me, and we both responded to the residence, and picked up the three boys. The 11-year-old girl was back at the residence with her brothers when I arrived. She said she was going to spend the night with a friend and she left the residence. The boys were inquisitive as to what was taking place but didn't show any reluctance when they were told what we were doing.

At approximately 1030 hours the following morning, the father of the four children contacted me at the police department and asked where his children were. I told him they were in a safe place and that they would be kept there until his girlfriend was sober and ready to take care of them. I told him I had removed the children under the direction of DFYS, after they were found to be alone, in a cold residence, and after we found they hadn't eaten. He told me there was food for them at the residence. I ask him how he knew, since he didn't live with them. The father told me this was none of my business, and he was getting angrier, and more argumentative. He demanded I tell him where his children were being housed. He was the type of man who intimidated and bullied people to get his way, but I was not one to be intimidated or bullied by him or anyone else. He made some statements that bordered on threats, and I told him he would be arrested if he continued to interfere. He said I was out of line, and I told him his children were wards of the state at this time, and I would arrest him for custodial interference if he took any actions at all regarding this matter. I guess he could sense the sincerity in my voice because he then left, muttering something under his breath.

At approximately 1330 hours the following afternoon, the mother of the children showed up and she was not too intoxicated, so I told her where the children were and why they were there. I told her she would have to leave the children where they were until DFYS said otherwise. She said they were her children and no one had any right taking them. I told her they hadn't eaten, and the house was filthy, and without any heat, and that an 11-year-old girl is not old enough to be left in charge of the three boys. I told her the 11-year-old had stayed with friends and I told her where her three boys were. I also told her she could not take the children until DFYS gave her permission to because they were now wards of the state. She asked if she could go see her children, and I told her she could if she didn't make any trouble. She assured me there would be no trouble.

It turned out the mother did go to the safe home and asked to see her children; she demanded she be allowed to take her children with her. She was ordered to leave the premises but refused to go without her children. Not wanting to get into a full-blown fight, the man gave the lady her children and then he called the police department, telling me what had taken place. I responded and located the lady and her four children on Main Street. I told her the children were wards of the state and she could be arrested for custodial interference if she refused to turn them over to me. She demanded I produce papers, and I told her the directives came straight from DFYS and, being the weekend, the papers weren't drawn up yet. I told her she wouldn't get the kids back the next time I found them without someone caring for them. I told her I'd be in touch with her and for her to stay with her children.

I left the lady and the children and went to the office, where I called the DFYS officer and brought him up to speed on what had taken place. He told me to let the kids stay with the mother and to do a welfare check on them from time to time, and if they were again without any supervision, I was to pull them and place them in a safe home again. He said he'd be in touch on Monday. He said he'd be coming over to meet with the parents of the children sometime during the first of the week.

The DFYS officer did come to town on Tuesday and met with the mother of the children. After his initial visit, he returned to Homer to address the court. He returned on Friday of the same week, and the children were taken out of the home and placed in foster care.

This case was very troubling to me because I knew all parties involved and I had no doubt the mother loved her children, but I fear she loved alcohol more. When the DFYS officer came on his second visit, the mother was intoxicated, and this was the determining factor for the DFYS Officer. He told me after he found the mother intoxicated again, he had no choice but to find a decent home for the children.

Love, in my opinion, is the most important factor in raising children, but, even though it's vitally important, other needs have to be met as well. When alcohol becomes so indoctrinated into a household, a lot of bad things can, and do, happen. The first thing to see to, in raising any child, is that child's safety and welfare. I hope this lady got her priorities straightened out and got her children back, but she moved from Seldovia, and I lost track of her. I'm sure the children were much better off after we intervened, but I hate to see it come to the place where separation of a family has to take place. (Case Closed by Referral to DFYS)

Ripping Off the Seldovia Harbor

On September 9, 1985, at approximately 0218 hours, the Seldovia Police Department received a report from the Homer dispatch that a boat owner, moored in the Seldovia Harbor, called and reported he had been sleeping aboard his vessel when he heard a noise that awakened him. He said a man going through items on his boat. He told the dispatcher he yelled at the man, asking him what he was doing on his boat, and the man fled. Officer Lewis and Officer Bishop, a part time officer who was sworn in to help out when needed, responded to the complainant's boat and spoke with him in person. The complainant gave a general description of the man and told them he was a blonde-haired man, approximately five feet six or five feet seven tall and that he was wearing a yellow hat. He said the man had a carton of cigarettes in his hand when he yelled at him. He said he startled the subject who threw the cigarettes down and ran off the boat. The complainant said he pursued the suspect and when he went onto the float, he observed another man 20 to 30 yards behind his boat. He asked the man if he'd seen the intruder leave his boat, and the man told him he didn't see anyone. The complainant found this odd, because the man who left his boat had run right past him. The complainant said he then spotted the man going up the ramp and he ran after him. He said he couldn't find him when he got ashore, and he went to a friend's home, and called 911. He further told the officers that when he was returning to his boat, he spotted the suspect again, and he was going aboard a vessel in the harbor. He told the officers the name of the boat.

Officer Lewis and Officer Bishop, with the complainant accompanying them, went aboard the boat where the suspect was said to have gone. Officer Lewis knocked on the door, and someone told them to come in. The officers found one man sitting at the table and another in a bunk. The officers requested identification of the two parties and, after they were identified, they were questioned by Officer Lewis. The complainant said the man at the table was the man who he'd seen just aft of his boat, when he was searching for the intruder. The man who was in the bunk was a blonde-haired man, who was approximately the same height as the intruder, but the complainant could not positively identify him as the man he saw aboard his boat. Both subjects denied any knowledge of anyone aboard the complainant's boat. The officers left the boat and went to the Seldovia Police Department. The two men aboard the vessel were run through the APSIN system, and the man sitting at the table had a warrant for his arrest for not appearing on a traffic ticket.

Officers Lewis and Bishop went back to the boat and arrested the subject who had the warrant. They transported him to the police department, where a booking sheet was filled out, and he was fingerprinted. His bail was $28 and, after signing a "Promise to Appear" form for a later date in Kenai, the subject was interviewed. He signed his "Waiver of Rights," and when Officer Lewis started questioning him, he stated there were two outboard motors hidden aboard the boat he was working on. One was in a tote and the other was in the forepeak of the vessel. He described a 2.2 hp Mercury outboard and a 15 hp Johnson outboard, which were taken off a boat which he named. He said they also took a set of tools, and he named the boat the tools were taken off of. He said a red six-gallon gas tank was set on the edge of one boat, which probably fell overboard and was floating in the harbor. He said a pair of side-cutters, a pair of plyers, a pair of gloves, and a toolbox were taken. He said he and his co-worker had gone aboard five boats in total and he said he had reported all the items they had taken.

The other deckhand on the boat was brought to the Seldovia Police Department while his friend was being detained; he was given his Miranda rights warning and he signed a "Waiver of Rights" form. He was interviewed by Officer Lewis and, after some time, he admitted to being involved in the taking of the items his co-worker had mentioned. Officer Lewis told him he thought he would apply for a search warrant and check the boat for other stolen items. The suspect told him his skipper would be really mad, and he'd probably lose his job if the police did that. Officer Lewis told him he thought he was holding out on him and he felt they had more items than he'd named so, the only way to be certain, was to search the vessel. The suspect told him he would get all the items back to him if he would not get the search warrant.

Officers Lewis and Bishop accompanied both subjects to their boat, and all the items listed, except for the gloves, were found and given to the officers. The officers made them take the items back to the vessels they had taken them from and put them back. After the items were returned, both suspects were arrested for felony theft and taken back to the police department. The two men were complaining about being arrested and it costing them their jobs. They asked if they could be released with a promise to appear at a later date. Officer Lewis called the court, and it was decided the two could be released on their promise to appear, and a date and time were scheduled. The two were told there would be arrest warrants issued if they failed to appear for their court hearing. They both assured the officers that they would not miss their court date. After signing "Promise to Appear" forms, both suspects were released and told if any more items came up missing, they would both be held in jail until their court dates. They said they were going to stay aboard the boat.

All the stolen items were returned to the owners. Even the gas tank, which was found floating in the harbor, was returned to the man who owned it. Officers Lewis and Bishop did a great job solving these thefts and, because of their work, all the victims got their items returned, and the two suspects were held responsible for their crimes. (Case Closed by Arrest)

1986: STATISTICS

I n 1986, the Seldovia Police Department again stayed busy. Three disorderly conduct charges were investigated, two civil disputes were investigated, two warrant arrests were conducted, one criminal mischief was reported and investigated, seven misdemeanor thefts and one felony theft were investigated, we responded to one automobile accident with injuries, five people were written citations for driving with license revoked, one child abuse and one child neglect case were investigated, one criminal trespass, three assaults, and three burglaries were investigated. Three negligent driving citations were issued, one misuse of plates citation was written, one sexual abuse of a minor investigation was conducted, three minors were charged with possession of alcohol, two death investigations were conducted, one sexual assault was charged, and one misconduct involving a controlled substance arrest was made. In addition, the city dock sustained damage when an Alaska state ferry, the Tustumena, was docking; an investigation was conducted and a subsequent report was given to the city manager.

Most of the investigations had to be done during normal working hours, and with Officer Lewis working nights, I was tasked with the majority of the investigations and report writing. I enjoyed the work, but it did become overwhelming at times. I also was pulled into a lot of the city's political problems and that was, by far, the worst part of the job. It seemed every time a new council member was elected, or a new city manager came on board, they brought with them a new set of political problems. I didn't feel I had time for the politics of the city and I felt I was drawn into it, on many occasions, just because the person requiring my input wanted an ally. I tried, unsuccessfully I'm afraid, to distance myself from this rhetoric. It became so bad at times that my wife and my daughter encouraged me to quit and find other employment. I knew I'd be out on a crab boat or on the North Slope in the oil fields or on a construction job again, and be away from home, so I endured a lot that I should never have had to be part of. As stated, politics were by far the worst part of the job.

SEXUAL ABUSE OF A MINOR REPORTED

At approximately 1040 hours on January 10, 1987, I was called by the Homer police dispatch, the 911 operator for our area, and I was told a 16-year-old girl had reported to a school counselor that she had been sexually assaulted on two occasions by her stepfather. I responded to the Susan B. English School and interviewed the girl in the principal's office. The young lady told me she had been sexually assaulted on two occasions by her stepfather and that the first time it happened was when her mother was out with friends. She said her stepfather sexually assaulted her in the living room on the couch on the first occasion. The second time, the sexual assault had occurred in her bedroom. Again, her mother was away, and she and her stepfather were the only two who were home. When I asked what was said by her stepfather she stated he told her not to tell anyone. I asked what she thought would happen if he found out she did tell others. She said she was afraid of him and didn't know what he would do, but he did have a temper. I asked if he'd ever hit her in the past, and she said he'd yelled at her and punched her in the shoulder one time but, other than that, he had not done more than yell. I asked if her stepfather had ever touched her inappropriately, and she said he had been touching her breasts under her shirt on a number of different occasions and that he had felt her privates on three occasions. When I inquired as to who else she had told about the sexual assault and sexual abuse, she said she hadn't told anyone before going to the school counselor. I did get more in-depth in the interview as to what actually occurred, and she provided a detailed account of the assaults.

Following the interview with the victim, I contacted DFYS (Division of Family & Youth Services), and, under their direction, arrangements were made to fly the victim to Homer, to a safe home. Both the DFYS officer and I agreed that getting the girl out of Seldovia was imperative.

I interviewed the counselor at the school and I also interviewed the principal. Both had interviewed the victim prior to contacting me, and I wanted to find out if they had been told anything that I had not been told. Both men pretty much were told the same thing the victim told me. I did request that, in future cases, if they called the police, to let us interview anyone making a report of sexual abuse because we didn't want to get a rehearsed statement from a victim or a suspect, and the more someone tells a story, the more they tend to stick to the rehearsed version, and might leave out vital information. Both men said they understood and said they would call immediately following any reports in the future.

After I had delivered the victim to the airport, and she had boarded an airplane to Homer, I called the suspect and had him come to the police department. When he arrived, I told him of the allegations and then I read him his Miranda warning. He signed the "Waiver of Rights," and I interviewed him. He adamantly denied ever touching his stepdaughter in a sexual manner and stated he had never forced himself on her in any way, sexually or otherwise. He said he wondered why she would make such an outlandish statement. He said he thought they were getting along well and didn't see this coming at all. When I asked if he could have inadvertently touched her breast or put his hand in the area of her genitals, something she might interpret differently than he did, he said there was no way anything like that could have happened. I asked him if his wife was away from the home on the dates in question. He said he didn't' remember on the first date it was alleged but said she was away from the home on the second occasion, but he again adamantly denied any form of sexual involvement with his stepdaughter.

I informed the suspect that we had taken his stepdaughter out of town and that she was in a safe home in Homer. He said that was good because, after this, she could not come back there. I told him I didn't know yet what would take place in this case, but I would keep him informed as it progressed. Before he left, he said if she wanted out of the house so badly, she could have just asked and they could have made arrangements to send her to her biological father's home or her older sister's. She didn't have to pull a stunt like this, he said. He told me he thought she was saying this just to get out of the house.

I next called the mother of the victim and had her come to the police department. Upon her arrival, I told her of the allegations, and she immediately said she didn't believe it. I inquired if she was away from the home on the two days in question, and she said she was, but she said she still didn't believe a word of it. She said on the last day in question, she and the suspect had had sexual relations the night before and she didn't think he would want to have sex the following morning. I asked her why she thought, if it was not true, that her daughter would make up the stories. She said she couldn't understand why she would say such a thing other than her wanting to get out of their home. She had talked about moving to the lower 48 with her older sister or her father, but she had never insisted on it. She seemed to only wonder if it was possible in the future, she said. I asked how the suspect and the victim got along, and she told me they didn't have a lot of problems, but her husband was always insisting the victim clean up her room and help around the house. She said she was a typical teenager, not wanting to do anything but be on the phone or watch television.

A trained sexual assault investigator re-interviewed the victim at the Homer Police Department, and the interview lasted for a couple hours. He had requested my report, including the interview with all the parties involved. After a lot of questioning and, after bringing anatomically correct dolls into play, the victim finally told the officer she wasn't sexually assaulted by her stepfather. She said she didn't get along well with the suspect and she wanted to get out of the home, but they didn't want her to go so, she thought by her telling us she was sexually assaulted, she would be sent to her father or to her older

sister's home in the States. She was admonished for her false reporting of such a serious matter but she was not charged. She was sent
stateside and is now living with her father, so she did accomplish what
she wanted. She was told that she was very lucky that charges were
not brought against her and that the officer would see to it that the
Children Services, where she was going, would be receiving a copy
of the case for future references. She was also told that her credibility
was now in question so anything like this, in the future, would most
probably not be taken too seriously.

It goes without saying that the suspect, and his wife, were very
relieved to hear the case had been dropped and that his stepdaughter
had admitted he had not sexually assaulted her.

This type of case is very difficult because it is difficult to interrogate
a victim. We tend to believe these types of allegations in that they are,
for the most part, true. A lot of children are sexually assaulted and/
or sexually abused, and the crimes are never reported. I understand
a few discrepancies in the girl's statement, after comparing it to my
interview with her, is what the officer picked up on, which convinced
him that the allegations were not true. I was glad to have all the help
I could get in these cases and I learned a lot by being involved in this
one. I just feel for the stepfather and the girl's mother for what they
must have gone through.

Interviews and interrogations are very different. The interview is a
preliminary finding of what is alleged to have taken place. Through
this process, a trained officer gets the feel for whether the victim is
truthful in their allegations. Interrogation takes place following the
collection of information, wherein the officer leads the process. In
interrogations, the officer is pretty well convinced as to what the truth
is by questioning the victim or suspect in a way that will bring out the
truth. As stated, we tend to believe the victims until we have evidence
that they are not being truthful. Interviewing victims of sexual assault
can be challenging. I found that I continued to learn and improve this
skill throughout my career. (Case Closed by Investigation)

A Memorable Wedding

One of the reasons I enjoyed being a police officer was due to the variety of incidents we became involved in. Some were certainly dangerous while many were somewhat mundane and not too exciting. However, in their own way, even the mundane cases were as important as were the more serious ones. Every once in a while, though, something would come along that was totally different from the normal calls we receive. I had one such call from a person I never would have ever believed would make such a request of me.

There was a couple who lived together here in town for many years but had never married. She was a very tall lady, possibly six feet one", and she had a very deep voice. He was probably five feet eight tall, with a frail build. The police were called to their residence frequently on domestic violence reports. It was not uncommon to arrest one or the other on DV assault charges after we arrived, so we were very well acquainted with both parties. Alcohol was always the common denominator. So, to say I was shocked when the man called and requested this of me would be a gross understatement. The man asked me if I would perform a marriage ceremony for him and his girlfriend. I told him I'd be honored to officiate at their wedding, and he told me of his plans. He had the day already picked and he had lined up witnesses. He said he wanted to have the ceremony at the Outside Beach Park.

I don't know about other states, but in Alaska, you can get what is called a "Commissioner for a Day" license to actually officiate at a wedding, and it's legal and binding once you pronounce them man and wife. Anyone can obtain the license and you don't have to hold a government office to be eligible.

I got all the information and I filled out the application paperwork needed by the court to issue the license allowing me to marry the two. So, everything was set, but when I got up on Saturday morning, the day they had picked for their wedding day, it was raining cats and dogs. To even think of having a wedding outdoors was out of the question. I called the man and asked him what he wanted to do. He said we had to have the ceremony on that day because he was retired out of the military and, if they weren't married on that date, his soon-to-be wife could not be added to his military insurance policy. He said there was no way he could wait. He said he didn't care if we had the ceremony in the police department, but it had to be done today. He told me, if I didn't mind, they would meet me at the police department at 1300 hours and they would have their witnesses with them so they could be married. I told him I was up for it if that was what he wanted to do, and the decision was made.

At 1300 hours, the man and his soon-to-be wife, along with their witnesses, arrived at the police department, and I performed the marriage ceremony. It was cramped in my office, to say the least, but they didn't seem to mind. When I pronounced them man and wife, I told him he could kiss his bride. She bent down and he kissed her. As soon as the kiss ended, she looked down at him and, in her deep voice, she said, "This is the first time we've ever been in here that we haven't been booked." Of course, everyone present had a good laugh, and I turned to the groom and told him, "Booked? Man, don't you realize? I've just given you a life sentence?" Of course, that brought on another round of laughter. I then signed the marriage license and made a copy and they left, off to the bar, to celebrate. When they walked out the door, I was thinking, "I'll see you later on tonight when you two get into another squabble."

Even after all my negative contacts with these two people, we remained friends. After a year or so had gone by, I asked the groom why, of all the people who could have married them, he had asked that I perform the ceremony. He said they knew I was just doing my job when I came to their home and he said I'd treated them with respect, so they held no hard feelings. I have to say I was quite flattered by this. Even more noteworthy is the fact that from that day, until the day I retired, I never was called to their residence again on a domestic violence problem. Now I don't believe they changed their ways but, for whatever reason, I never got a call.

Once in a while, the job was very gratifying. You never do know how you are received when you are enforcing the rules and making arrests, but I found, if you treat everyone with respect, even when you are putting them in handcuffs, it will pay huge dividends in the end.

In my career, I married a total of eight couples. Each time I felt honored to have been asked to officiate at their weddings. (Case Closed by Performing a Wedding Ceremony

ASSAULT IN THE FOURTH DEGREE

On February 4, 1987, at approximately 0240 hours, I received a call from a lady stating the police were needed at her neighbor's home. The caller said the lady from next door had come to her home and had awakened her by pounding on the door. She said, when she answered the door, her neighbor was standing there nude and crying, telling her she needed help. The caller said the lady had been beaten up. I dressed quickly and responded to the caller's home, which was located in a trailer park. The lady in distress was contacted and was now dressed; she had a shoe on her right foot but none on her left foot. I observed her face to be swollen; it was starting to discolor and starting to show a bruise. Her left eye was blackened, but that appeared to be an old injury. She was intoxicated and she told me her boyfriend had bitten her on the face, on her lip, on her eyebrow, on her arm, on her breast, and in the area of her genitals. I immediately called the EMTs and questioned the victim while we were waiting for them to arrive. The victim stated her boyfriend had forced her to have sex prior to the assault and that he had attempted to cut her clothes off with a knife. She further said he had forced her to have sex with him a week before this had happened, on a Thursday.

The EMTs arrived and, after their examination of the victim, they transported her to the clinic where she could be examined by Dr. Larry Reynolds.

I attempted to find the suspect, but he was not home, and I was unable to locate him. I called John Gruber, a friend who always assisted me when I didn't have a patrol officer. I told him I needed help locating a suspect and that Officer Lewis was out of town. I then went to his residence and picked him up.

We searched for the suspect and finally located him hiding behind the trailer where he lived. I arrested him for assault in the fourth degree and placed him in handcuffs. We then transported him to the Seldovia Police Department. The suspect was highly intoxicated. Upon arriving at the police department, I read him his Miranda rights and he signed his "Waiver of Rights" form. I then interviewed him. I observed scratches on his arm and on his cheek, and he told me he needed to see the doctor. I told him the doctor was with his girlfriend, but I would have him come to the police department after he was finished with her.

During the interview, the suspect denied forcing his girlfriend to have sex with him and further denied trying to cut her pants off with a knife. He stated he didn't have a knife. He did admit to biting her in the face, on the eyebrow, on the lip, and in the genital area. He said the fight started after they had sex but he adamantly denied forcing her to have sex with him. I asked if he had ever forced her to have sex when she didn't want to, and he said he never forced her, or anyone, to have sex with him. The suspect was highly intoxicated and was argumentative, so I decided to wait until he sobered up to interview him further.

I called the doctor's office and told him I needed him to come to the police department to examine the suspect after he'd finished with the victim. He said he was about to conclude his examination of the girlfriend. Approximately half an hour later, the doctor arrived. He examined the suspect; he told me that the suspect only wanted to talk to him and that he wasn't injured, other than the scratches I had observed. He did persuade the suspect to have his degree of intoxication checked. I performed an intoximeter examination, which resulted in a blood alcohol of .171. Following the breath test, the suspect was placed in the jail cell. A jail guard was called and came to the police department to watch over the prisoner.

Officer Gruber and I went back to the victim's home, and I conduct-ed an in-depth interview with her. During this interview, she denied telling me that her boyfriend had attempted to cut her pants off of her. She further stated that he didn't force her to have sex with him, but she did say he'd bitten her on her eyebrow, on her lip, on her cheek, on her breast, and in the area of her genitals. Because of the inconsistency of her statement, I couldn't charge the suspect with sexual assault. The victim also told me she didn't want the suspect to go to jail. She said she loved him and he was the best thing that had ever happened to her. She had sobered up somewhat, and I tended to believe there was no sexual assault. She was just angry when I interviewed her while we were waiting for the EMTs to arrive.

I re-interviewed the suspect after he'd sobered up, and he still ada-mantly denied sexually assaulting his girlfriend. He did admit to biting her in all the aforementioned places on her body, so I charged him with assault in the fourth degree. At the arraignment, he pled no contest, and the magistrate found him guilty. He was sentenced to thirty days in jail with twenty days suspended. He was fined $500 with $500 suspended. He was ordered to go to SKIAP for alcohol screening and to adhere to any recommendations they had. He was also placed on probation for two years and ordered to abstain from consuming alcohol.

Given the inconsistency of the victim's statement, the physical as-sault is the only charge we could bring against the suspect. If you took alcohol out of the equation, the incident most probably would never have occurred, but that can be said about many of these cases. (Case Closed by Arrest)

LOST AT SEA

Over the years, since 1964 when I came to Alaska, I have lost many friends and acquaintances in fishing accidents that occurred while they were commercial fishing. Many have gone down with the vessel they were fishing on, and some have suffered life-threatening injuries. The incident I'm going to tell you about happened to a young man who, along with his family, was well-liked and respected in and around Seldovia. It was one of the most impacting losses this town has ever experienced.

On February 22, 1987, at approximately 2220 hours, while setting king crab pots approximately 12½ miles SE of Augustine Island, in the Kamashak Bay area, David Rodney Hilts was swept overboard by a rogue wave. He was fishing on the *F/V Alliance,* and the weather was inclement. The wave that washed David Hilts overboard also damaged crab pots that were on the deck, ripped a crab pot out of the launch rack from the hydraulic dogs locking it down, and washed another deckhand off his feet, pushing him under the launch rack. The first sighting of David was when he was seen approximately 100 yards off the starboard stern of the vessel. All attempts to rescue him were unsuccessful. A line was thrown to him, but he could not grab it. He disappeared beneath the vessel's bow and was then seen floating face down on the other side of the boat and was observed sinking beneath the water. The *Alliance* crew stayed on the fishing grounds and searched for the young man for hours, finally ending their search after 0200 hours on February 23. The boat then returned to its home port of Seldovia.

The Coast Guard was immediately notified, following the accident, and they conducted a thorough search of the area. Their search started on the morning of February 23, but they were unable to locate David as well. After utilizing all their resources and not finding the young man's remains, they called off their search.

At approximately 0930 hours, Gordon Giles, owner/operator of the *F/V Alliance*, contacted me and reported the incident to me. I interviewed Mr. Giles on record at the Seldovia Police Department, and he stated that they were setting king crab pots approximately 12½ miles southeast of Augustine Island, and the wind was blowing approximately 35–40 mph out of the northeast. He said there was a confused sea. A swell was coming from the southeast and they were setting with the swell on the port quarter stern when a large swell came across the deck from the port side. Mr. Giles told me he was below deck when the incident occurred, and his son, Mark, was running the boat. Mark Immediately called him to the bridge following the accident. He said he told Mark to keep sight of David, who was on the starboard stern of the vessel, while he turned around to come alongside him so they could throw him a lifeline. When they came alongside him, the crew threw him a line, but he was unable to grab it. The wind caught the bow of the boat, and Mr. Giles said he tried to twin-screw the vessel to avoid drifting over David, but the wind caught the boat, and he watched David disappear beneath the bow. Gordon said they continued to search for David until 0200 hours the next morning, before giving up the search and returning to Seldovia. He said it was not unusual to fish in that kind of weather but it was unusual to get a wave like that washing the deck. He said a freak wave came across the deck and washed David overboard

Mr. Giles was very distraught and visibly shaken, and I could feel his pain. David Hilts was the son of longtime friends of Mr. Giles's, and they had attended the same church together for many years. He told me it was as if he'd lost a family member.

Following my interview with Gordon Giles, I interviewed his son, Mark, and Eric Haugstad, Brian Rhor, and Thor Burt, the crew members who were aboard the vessel and witnesses to the accident. All those I interviewed said basically the same thing about how the rogue wave washed the deck and created havoc, washing David overboard. It had also washed Brian Rhor under the launch rack, ripped the pot loose on the launch rack, and damaged pots that were stacked on deck. Eric Haugstad stated he was on top of the stack of pots, when the wave came across the deck, and all he could do was hold on and watch what happened on deck. Each crew member I interviewed was physically shaken by the event and all showed remorse.

The *Alliance* was a 100-foot king crab fishing vessel, and they regularly fished in the type of weather they experienced that day. It was a typical winter storm that is a frequent event in the area. The area is renowned for its bad weather but also was known to be an area with good king crab fishing.

On February 17, after the Coast Guard had suspended the search for David Hilts, Jim Hopkins, Jesse Boothe, pilot Larry Thompson and I flew for two and a half hours, searching for the remains of David Hilts. We wanted so badly to bring the young man home so the family could have closure, but we were unable to locate him.

The family was given permission by the city of Seldovia to erect a memorial in honor of David Hilts at the Outside Beach Park. On a knoll overlooking Kachemak Bay, Lower Cook Inlet, and the Kamashak Bay area, they built a bench out of cement and had a plaque made to honor David. We all go there, from time to time, to pay our respects to the memory of a wonderful young man who was taken from us way too soon. Rest in peace David Hilts. You are missed. (Case Closed by Investigation)

A Suspicious Boat Sinking

On March 17, 1987, at approximately 0740 hours, I received a call from a David Bishop, reporting that his boat had sunk during the night and he suspected foul play. David was a personal friend and a man who at times acted as a patrol officer when help was needed.

I had been aboard his boat the previous day, following David purchasing it. It was a local Homer boat built by George Hamm. It was a 28-foot-long vessel; it had a forward cabin and a fish hold, and it was powered by an inboard engine. The boat was commonly known as a Hamm Hull. They were very well-built vessels made from a fiberglass mold.

David said he'd gotten a call from the harbor master, who had found the boat sunk in the harbor. A diver, Dean Ihrie, was summoned to dive and place lines around the vessel so we could bring it up. When the lines were in place, we raised the boat with the rigging from a large crab fishing vessel. We would pick the boat up where the deck was above the waterline and then pump the water out of it. Repeated efforts in this way raised the boat and, once it floated, I brought the Public Safety Boston Whaler alongside and moved it to the boat launch ramp, where it could be put on a trailer and pulled out of the water.

After the boat was pulled out of the water, we checked the bottom for any holes that would explain why the boat had sunk. Finding none, we asked questions of people who were in the harbor during the night, but no one had observed anyone around the vessel.

On the previous evening, before leaving the boat, David had pumped what little water was in the bilge overboard. Because the exhaust hose was trailed off the transom of the boat and was in the water, we surmised that a back siphon had occurred and filled the boat with water, causing it to sink. I had witnessed this happen to larger boats than this one and, on each occasion, it was following the bilge being pumped and the exhaust hose, or through-hull fitting, being below the waterline, due to a list in the vessel. This is not something one would think of unless they had experienced it in the past, but we were convinced that is what happened, causing Mr. Bishop's boat to sink.

The engine was quickly flushed out with fresh water, and David cleaned up the vessel. The boat was again used after the sinking, and no further problems of this nature occurred, so we were satisfied that that was what had happened.

I put this story in the book so those reading it would know not be caught in the same situation, and to make sure to remove any exhaust hose from the water after pumping the bilge. You should also make sure the through-hull fitting, for the bilge exhaust, is not below the waterline due to a list, or the leaning to one side, of a vessel. This will also often create a back-siphon if it's beneath the waterline.

See, my book isn't just entertaining, it's educational, as well. (Case Closed by Investigation)

Murder in the Second Degree

On June 6, 1987, at approximately 0245 hours, Officer Jerry Lewis received a call from a man, reporting there had been a stabbing at the cannery crew bunkhouse, in Room #7. The caller told Officer Lewis that the suspect, a female, had come pounding on his door and that she was hysterical. He said she told him she had just stabbed her boyfriend. The caller said she was flipping out and he was having a hard time getting her to explain what had taken place. Officer Lewis told the caller to keep the suspect at his residence and the police would be there soon. As soon as the caller hung up, Officer Lewis called Officer John Gruber and asked that he respond to the cannery trailers to keep anything more from happening and to secure the scene. I was out of Seldovia at the time and couldn't be of any assistance in the investigation.

Officer Gruber responded, and Officer Lewis told him the original caller said the stabbing had occurred in Room #7 at the cannery housing units. Officer Gruber went to the trailer and found the door of Room #7 to be open; he observed a male lying on the bed. The man was wearing a white tee shirt, which was covered with blood on the front, in the area of his heart and sternum. The man was conscious and said his girlfriend had stabbed him and he pointed to a knife on the floor, indicating that it was the weapon she used. Officer Gruber picked up the knife, being careful not to get his fingerprints on it, and secured it. He told the victim the EMTs had been dispatched. A male

EMT showed up before the others, having driven his own vehicle to the scene. He entered the room and started talking with the victim. Officer Gruber stayed on the scene and waited until Officer Lewis arrived.

Officer Gruber gave Officer Lewis the knife and told him what he had observed thus far. He pointed out where the weapon had been lying when he retrieved it. Officer Lewis put the knife in an envelope and then placed it in his vehicle. Officer Gruber was directed to stay with the victim while Officer Lewis contacted the suspect.

The ambulance and EMT crew arrived on the scene and immediately went to work on the victim. They placed a bandage over the wound and cleaned the blood off the victim. Dr. Larry Reynolds arrived shortly after that and also examined the victim. A medevac had already been ordered and the airplane would be landing in approximately an hour.

Officer Lewis contacted the suspect at the home of the original caller, and she was still hysterical. She kept stating she had stabbed her boyfriend and probably killed him. She repeatedly said she didn't mean to stab him, but he had burned her children's pictures. After she calmed down, Officer Lewis told her she would have to come down to the police department. The EMTs had the victim loaded and were transporting him to the airport. Officer Lewis secured the victim's room, placed a padlock on the door, and put some crime scene tape across the entrance. He then told Officer Gruber to meet him at the police department. Officer Lewis then loaded the suspect into the patrol vehicle and transported her to the police department. Upon reaching the department, the suspect was asked to have a seat facing the desk. She was then given her Miranda warning, and she signed the "Waiver of Rights" form. The suspect smelled of alcohol and showed signs of intoxication.

Officer Lewis advised the suspect that the conversation would be recorded and then he asked her to explain, in her own words, what had taken place at the apartment when she stabbed her boyfriend. She told the officer that she and her boyfriend had been arguing and they had gone to the Knight Spot Bar. They had a couple drinks and then an argument ensued. The victim slapped her, and the bartender came over and told him he had to leave. He left the bar, and she stayed to finish her drink. She then left and went to the Seldovia Lodge. The victim was at the Lodge and they had a couple more beers together. The suspect said she had gone to the bathroom and had left her wallet on the table. The victim had picked it up and, when she returned, he refused to give it back to her. The suspect told Officer Lewis they had a few more beers and then they went home. The victim still wouldn't give her the wallet. She said he told her he was going to burn her children's pictures.

She told the officer she didn't have anything else of her children's, except the pictures, and the victim knew how much they meant to her. She said they were both intoxicated when they got home; the victim took the pictures out of the wallet and then threw the wallet at her. He then burned the pictures and put them in the ashtray while they were burning. She said she was mad. She had to use the bathroom and while in there, she observed a filet knife in the dish rack. They didn't have a sink, so she did the dishes in the bathtub, she said. She picked up the knife and walked out of the bathroom and stabbed the victim. She said she had just wanted him to hurt and that she wasn't trying to stab him in a certain place, just somewhere where it would hurt. He had beaten her in the past on a number of different occasions and had put her in the hospital on one occasion. He had been arrested for assaulting her on three separate occasions, but in each case, she would drop the charges, she said. He beat her once for three days and when he burned the pictures of her children, she said that was the last straw.

Dr. Larry Reynolds called Officer Lewis at the police department and told him that the victim had died when being transported to Homer. It was no longer a felony assault; it was now a homicide. Officer Lewis made the suspect aware that her boyfriend had died and that she would be charged with murder in the second degree. He then called the Alaska State Troopers, and they began making arrangements to come to Seldovia and take over the investigation when there was enough daylight to fly.

Officer Lewis booked the suspect and placed her in a jail cell. She was again hysterical after hearing that her boyfriend had succumbed due to her stabbing him. She was sobbing when the officer placed her in the jail cell. Officer Lewis called a lady to guard the suspect, and she arrived approximately half an hour later.

At approximately 0930 hours, Officer Lewis picked up Trooper Bartolini and Trooper Weatherly at the Seldovia Airport. He took the two troopers to the scene of the crime; he unlocked the door and removed the crime scene tape so they could gain entry. Trooper Bartolini had a search warrant with him for the room. Trooper Weatherly drew a diagram of the floor plan of the room and listed all the contents in the room. The bedding, the blood-soaked tee shirt, and other items were tagged, bagged, and taken as evidence. The weapon used was already in the evidence locker at the Seldovia Police Department. Measurements were made, and numerous photographs were taken of the interior of the unit. After approximately two hours, the door to the room was again padlocked, and the crime scene tape was again placed over the entrance.

`Officer Lewis transported the troopers to the Seldovia Police Department, where Trooper Bartolini interviewed the suspect. He again gave her the Miranda rights warning, and she signed another "Waiver of Rights" form. The trooper told her the interview would be tape-recorded. The suspect told the trooper basically the same things she had told Officer Lewis, but she brought out more times that she had been beaten by the victim. She said she'd had her ribs broken on one occasion but, when she'd gone to the hospital for treatment, she'd told them she'd fallen down a flight of stairs. She told Trooper Bartolini that she wasn't trying to kill her boyfriend, only to make him hurt because he was always hurting her. She broke down again, and the interview had to be suspended for a time. Trooper Bartolini was very thorough and got all the information he needed from her.

Throughout the day, numerous people were called down to the police department and were interviewed on record by both Trooper Bartolini and Trooper Weatherly. The people in the bar who had witnessed the assault by the victim when he was kicked out of the Knight Sports Bar. Anyone who was mentioned that had contact with the two during the evening leading up to the event. All the EMTs who'd responded to the call and were at the scene. Officers Lewis and Officer

Gruber, the man who gave the couple a ride home from the Seldovia Lodge, and the bartenders at both bars were all interviewed on tape. After the troopers were satisfied that they had everything they needed, an airplane was ordered to take them and the suspect to Homer.

Officer Lewis provided transportation for the troopers and the prisoner to the Seldovia Airport, and they boarded a Cook Inlet Aviation plane and departed.

The case dragged on for a long time, and the suspect spent a lot of time in jail awaiting trial. She was indicted on charges of murder in the second degree and she could not make bail. When the judgment did come down, the lady was treated with leniency in that they had ruled she was a battered woman and she was given a sentence which everyone felt was just. She was released and was sentenced to the time served, and she was placed on probation for five years. She was also ordered to undertake alcohol treatment and not to consume alcoholic beverages to excess.

NOTE: This sentence was passed on to me and was third party information, so it may be different from what actually was ordered. I never did receive a disposition form on this case, so I am only passing on the information I was given by another officer who did follow the case.

When I returned to work, I reviewed the case and I was proud of how the Seldovia police officers had responded and handled the case. They were thorough, respectful, and professional throughout the investigation. Seldovia was well served by Officer Jerry Lewis and Officer John Gruber. (Case Closed by Arrest)

With that, I will call this book finished. I do hope you enjoyed walking through these first eight years of my police career with me. I made a lot of mistakes over the years, when I was trying to learn what it takes to be a bush cop in Seldovia, Alaska. The first few years were certainly the most difficult but, in the police profession, one never quits learning. The laws keep changing with every legislative session, and the criminals keep developing new ways to circumvent the law, so the learning curve is never-ending. It keeps the job interesting. Unlike in larger communities, the Alaska bush cops deal mostly with people they are acquainted with and/or have a personal relationship with. In my view, it would be much easier to police a community where you were not acquainted with anyone, where everyone you dealt with was a complete stranger. But there is a very definite need for bush cops throughout Alaska, and I am proud to have served the Seldovia area for nearly thirty-two years as their chief of police.

I hope you'll join me in my next addition of *Alaska Bush Cop*. We will share many more of the exciting activities of the Seldovia Police Department. I hope to have the next book out in the spring of 2020, so be watching for it.

Ramblings of an
Alaskan Bush Poet
A Common Man's Stories Through Rhyme

A.W. "Andy" Anderson

I've held a myriad of jobs in the more than 53 years I've made Alaska, the Great Land, my home. Varieties of employment, along with my other life experiences, have given me an interesting and exciting existence. My experiences have been educational, some frightening, some life threatening, some humorous, some heartbreaking, but all played a part in preparing me for the writing of Ramblings of an Alaskan Bush Poet. I'm hopeful my backstories will put the reader in somewhat the same mind set, or emotion, I was experiencing at the time. When readers discuss my work I hope to be viewed as a common man who tells his stories through rhyme and, at the same time, someone who paints a vivid picture of what my limericks convey.

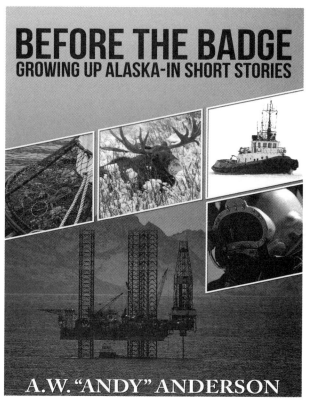

BEFORE THE BADGE
GROWING UP ALASKA-IN SHORT STORIES

A.W. "ANDY" ANDERSON

At 16 years of age I quit school and moved to Alaska. I was a kid in a man's world and for the next 15 years I took on a myriad of jobs to survive. I had some harrowing experiences and I lived a very exciting life during that time period. Being born on a farm, I was introduced to the operation of equipment at a very young age and I found myself working in jobs that involved machinery and its operation. In 1979 I became a Police Officer and my career lasted nearly 32 years. The seven short stories in Before The Badge outline many of my life's experiences between 1964 and 1979. It tells of a young man's life as he is becoming a man and, when doing so, gets involved in many things which are educational, exciting and at times, life threatening. The seven stories are all true.